The Jungle Grammar Teacher and Parent Guide

KENNA BOURKE

Oxford University Press 1997

Contents

Read this before you start! 3

Notes on The Jungle Grammar Book 1 4

Notes on The Jungle Grammar Book 2 24

How to play the games 44

A glossary of activities 46

Read this before you start!

To the teacher

This guide is intended to provide you with ideas for the exploitation of *The Jungle Grammar Books 1 & 2*. In it you will find hundreds of suggestions as to how to make the best use of the students' books. There are five things you should know before you turn over this page:

1 The books are divided into ten chapters. Each chapter starts with a double page showing how a grammatical structure is used. The following two pages provide oral and written exercises on that structure. There are also two games in the students' books, one in the middle and one at the end.

2 The way you decide to use the Jungle Books is entirely your affair. The ideas you will find in this guide are suggestions only. Each chapter in the Guide is divided into sections. Here is an explanation of each of them. **Words** comprises words that are in the text of the students' book and, on occasion, some words which I thought you might find useful in addition. Words which appear in word lists of previous chapters are not repeated in subsequent chapters. **Questions to ask children** are prompts which you might use when the children look at the picture for the first time. You may decide to use the children's mother tongue or English, depending on your assessment of your class's ability. **Just for fun** is simply that: a diversion for when your children are in need of a break. **Exercises** are described as being written, oral or both. There is always an extra activity to back up the exercise. Answers are also provided. **Other things to do** is divided into quick and long activities. These provide ideas for developing the chapter further. It would also be worth your looking at the section entitled **Parents**. Many of these activities may be adapted for use in class. This symbol ◉ indicates that an activity is not suitable for parents.

3 Almost every page in the books can be used for a variety of purposes, irrespective of what the grammar topic happens to be. Look, for instance, at Chapter 2 of Book 1, pages 8–9. Here are a few things you could teach using the picture only: present continuous, prepositions of place, questions, short answers, colours, counting, adjectives, present simple of **be**, possessives, **I like** and **I don't like**.

4 The red lizard is a mischievous character who appears on every double page but one of each book. Ask the children to look for him on every page.

5 Smuff is my rabbit. He has asked me to say that he solemnly promises to write to any child who writes to him. He has never yet broken a promise.

I hope that you and your children will have fun using the books. Grammar need not be a nasty-tasting medicine!

To the parent

This guide is intended to provide you with ideas for the exploitation of *The Jungle Grammar Books 1 & 2*. In it you will find hundreds of suggestions for making the best use of the students' books. There are five things you should know before you turn over this page:

1 The books are divided into ten chapters. Each chapter starts with a double page showing how a grammatical structure is used. The following two pages provide oral and written exercises on that structure. There are also two games in the students' books, one in the middle and one at the end.

2 The suggestions you will find in this guide are suggestions only. Each chapter in the Guide is divided into sections. Here is an explanation of each of them: **Words** comprises words that are in the text of the students' book and, on occasion, some words which I thought you might find useful in addition. Words which appear in word lists of previous chapters are not repeated in subsequent chapters. **Questions to ask children** are prompts which you might use when your child looks at the picture for the first time. You may decide to use your mother tongue or English, depending on your assessment of your child's ability. **Just for fun** is simply that: a diversion for when your child is in need of a break. **Exercises** are described as being written, oral or both. There is always an extra activity to back up the exercise. Answers are also provided. **Other things to do** is divided into quick, long and parent activities. These provide ideas for developing the chapter further. You can use everything in this book except for activities which have this symbol ◉ beside them. These are activities which require a number of children. You may, of course, find ways of adapting them to suit your own needs.

3 Almost every page in the books can be used for a variety of purposes, irrespective of what the grammar topic happens to be. Look, for instance, at Chapter 2 of Book 1, pages 8–9. Here are a few things you could practise using the picture only: present continuous, prepositions of place, questions, short answers, colours, counting, adjectives, present simple of **be**, possessives, **I like** and **I don't like**.

4 The red lizard is a mischievous character who appears on every double page but one of each book. Ask your child to look for him on every page.

5 Smuff is my rabbit. He has asked me to say that he solemnly promises to write to any child who writes to him. He has never yet broken a promise.

I hope that you and your child will enjoy using *The Jungle Grammar Books*. There is no longer any need for grammar to be a monster; it can actually be quite fun.

BOOK 1

Chapter 1 Present simple of **be**

Words

bird	friend	monkey	snake
butterfly	frog	name	spider
crocodile	giraffe	popcorn	tortoise
elephant	lion	rabbit	tree

Questions to ask children

Pages 4–5

- How many names of animals do you know?
- Can you make any animal noises?
- Which animal do you like best?
- What is a jungle?
- What is happening in the picture?
  The animals are watching a film of themselves.
- Can you point at the animal who is buying ice cream?
- Which animal is Mr Lion?
- Which is Mrs Lion?
- How can you tell the difference?

The write-in gaps left on pages 4–5 are not an exercise. Children decide for themselves what they want to call the animals. You can do this as a class, in pairs, or individually. Use either English names or the children's mother tongue, as you prefer, e.g. *Mr Charlie Crocodile*.

Just for fun

Ask the children to find these things:

A bird in a tree.
A duck taking a photograph.
A bird on a hippo's head.
A crocodile eating popcorn.

Can they see the red lizard?
He is tying the two monkeys' tails together.

Pages 6–7

- Can you find Mr and Mrs Crocodile?
- Which is which?
- How can you tell?
- Who is having a photograph taken?
- How many animals' photographs can you see?
- How many birds are in the picture?

Just for fun

Ask the children to find these things:

Tortoises playing a game.
A rabbit trying to catch a fly.
A monkey wearing a hat.
A butterfly.

Can they see the red lizard?
He is sticking his tongue out.

Exercise A

Written. Children fill in the gaps. Could also be done orally.

1 I'm a frog.
2 We're frogs.
3 I'm a monkey.
4 We're monkeys.
5 I'm a bird.
6 We're birds.

- Extra: ask the children to mime animals. They should do this individually to practise *I'm*, and in pairs to practise *We're*. The rest of the class guesses what they are 'saying', e.g. *I'm a monkey. We're giraffes.*

Exercise B

Oral. Children say their name and their friend's name. You can do this in two ways: either to practise *I'm* and *You're* or to practise *I'm* and *She's/He's*.

- Extra: play a game of Blind Man's Buff. Blindfold one child. Tell the others to keep absolutely silent. Tell the children to shake hands with the blindfolded child. He tries to guess who he is shaking hands with. He must say: *You're . . .*

Exercise C

Written. Children fill in the gaps. Could also be done orally.

1 He's Mr Rabbit.
2 She's Mrs Crocodile.
3 She's Mrs Monkey.
4 He's Mr Elephant.
5 She's Mrs Giraffe.

- Extra: use other pages in the book (e.g. pages 26–27) and ask the children to say who the animals are.

Exercise D

Oral. Children name the animals.

1 They're birds.
2 They're spiders.
3 They're snakes.
4 They're tortoises.

- Extra: point at other animals on this page or another in the book (e.g. 20 or 21). Ask: *What are they?*
  You can also do this with objects, e.g. *They're books.*

Other things to do

Quick activities

- Bring in or draw pictures of other animals or people and use them to practise *He's* and *She's*.
- ⊙ Play a chain game. Child 1 says his name: e.g. *I'm John.* Child 2 says: *He's John, I'm Peter.* Child 3 says: *He's John, he's Peter, I'm Mary* and so on.
- ⊙ Or make this more difficult by asking the children to invent false names for themselves.
- If animal vocabulary is new to the children, try introducing the names of animals with flashcards. Get children to draw their own cards, or write the names of animals on separate bits of card.
- If you do make animal flashcards, double each one and play Snap.
- Play Hangman on the board, using only the names of animals.
- Practise counting. Ask how many crocodiles, monkeys, frogs etc. there are. Pages 6–7 are good for numbers. See also pages 20–21.

Longer activities

- Miming game. Children mime an animal and others guess which one it is. They should say *You're a . . .* or *He's/She's a . . .*
- Play an 'In the Jungle' game. The first child says: *In the jungle I see a monkey.* Next child says: *In the jungle I see a monkey and an elephant . . .* etc.
- Try doing an animal alphabet on the board: **a** is for ant, **b** is for bear, **c** is for crocodile . . .
- ⊙ Divide the children into small groups. Ask each group to draw a set of animals, e.g. Group 1 draws five lions, Group 2 draws four monkeys. When they have finished, stick the drawings on a large sheet of paper. Fill any white space with jungle trees and flowers. Display the picture on the classroom wall.
- Play a guessing game. Tell the children to think of a character in the book or a famous person. They should try to say two sentences about the person, e.g. (Mr Crocodile) *I'm green. I'm big.* The class guesses who they are.
- ⊙ If you have a class that can be divided into pairs exactly, cut one slip of paper for each child. Divide the slips into two piles. Write the name of any animal that makes a noise on each of the slips. Do exactly the same for the second pile of papers, so that, for instance, you have two slips which are marked *Lion*, two that are marked *Dog* etc. Mix up all the pieces of paper and put them in a box. Tell each child to take one piece of paper. They should not show their piece of paper to anyone else. When you tell them to start, they should all make the noise of the animal on their paper and move round the classroom until they have found their partner.

Parents

- Cut pictures of men and women, boys and girls out of newspapers and magazines. Get your child to look at the pictures and practise saying, e.g. *He's a boy. She's a girl.*
- Make a list of ten animals, e.g. *monkey, crocodile, lion, elephant* etc. Cut up twenty pieces of paper or card. Make two identical sets of cards by writing the name of each animal on each piece of card. Shuffle the cards and play Snap with your child.
- Choose five letters of the alphabet. With your child, see how many animals you can think of for each letter.
- Extend the last activity by asking your child to draw an animal for each letter. Write the names of the animals under each picture. Put the pictures on your child's bedroom wall to remind him of the names of the animals.
- Practise counting. Use other pages in the book, e.g. pages 20–23, and help your child to count how many different animals there are.
- Get your child to draw or cut pictures out of magazines, e.g. *one lion, two dogs, three birds.* Make this into a number poster to put on the wall.
- Play a guessing game with your child. Think of a person you both know. Say two or three sentences about the person (in English or in your mother tongue). Your child guesses who it is you 'are'. He should say (in English): *You're . . .* Take turns to play the game.
- Go through the book looking for male and female animals. Encourage your child to say, e.g. *He's a monkey. She's a crocodile.*

BOOK 1

Chapter 2 Nouns and **a** or **an**

Words

apple	coconut	octopus	pineapple
banana	egg	orange	rug
book	football	owl	ruler
bottle	grape	pen	table
chair	melon	pencil	umbrella

Questions to ask children

Pages 8–9

- How many kinds of fruit can you name?
- What are your favourite fruits?
- What kind of fruit does a monkey like most?
- What is happening in the picture?
  It is market day. The animals are shopping.
- Who is buying an orange?
- Who is buying an apple?
- Who is selling umbrellas?
- Who is asleep?
- What other things are for sale in the market?
- If you were at the jungle market, what would you buy?

Just for fun

Ask the children to find these things:

A bird in the melons.
A bear kicking a football.
A rhinoceros juggling eggs.
A rabbit.
Two birds in two pots.
A tortoise.

Can they see the red lizard?
He's throwing eggs at Mrs Lion.

Pages 10–11

- What can you see in the picture?
- Is there a river?
- Is there a café?
- Have you been to a café?
- What is your favourite drink?
- How many animals are having a drink?
  Five, including the tortoise.
- Which animal has not been seen in the book before?
  The octopus.
- How many legs has an octopus got?

Just for fun

Ask the children to find these things:

A rabbit jumping into the water.
A monkey holding a glass with his feet.
A fish hiding behind the waterfall.
A bird in a tree.
A spider.
A blue bird.

Can they see the red lizard?
He's catapulting a stone from the riverbank.

Exercise A

Oral or written. Children follow the strings to find out what each animal has got.

The crocodile has got a football and a book.
The monkey has got an umbrella, a ruler and a banana.
The lion has got a book, a pen and an egg.
The bird has got an apple and an orange.

- Extra: bring in a set of objects, or pictures of objects, and give each child three or four of them. The rest of the class says what each child has got.

Exercise B

Oral or written. Children decide which pot the octopus should put the objects into. (Ask the children to draw lines on the book connecting the objects to the pots.)

A pineapple	An elephant
A banana	An owl
A pencil	An orange
A coconut	An apple
A ball	An egg
A bottle	

- Extra: play the same game on the board. Write words across the top of the board. Draw two boxes at the bottom of the board. Label one box **A** and the other **An**. Ask children to tell you which words go in which box. Draw lines to connect the words to the boxes, or write the words in the boxes.

Exercise C

Written. Children join the dots to form an elephant.

- Extra: it may be useful at this stage to revise numbers. Write numbers 1–45 on the board. Ask the children to say the numbers aloud as a class.

Exercise D

Oral or written. Children list the things they can remember from the picture. Suggested answers:

There is a fish, there is an owl, there is an octopus.

- Extra: organize a True or False game. Write several true and false sentences about the pictures in this chapter on the board, e.g. *There is an owl on page 8.* (False.) Children decide whether they are true or false.

Other things to do

Quick activities

- Revise the names of fruits using flashcards or real examples.
- Bring in several objects and put them in a bag. Get the children to feel them and guess what they are.
- Play a memory game: put a number of objects on the desk, allow the children to study them for a minute or so, then take one object away. The children say what's missing.
- ◉ Ask children to draw objects of their choosing on the blackboard. The class guesses what they are.
- Tell the children to look at pages 8 and 9. Ask them to tell you what the other characters might be saying, e.g. *Mr Monkey, the two birds in the pots, Mr Rhino.*

Longer activities

- Introduce **I like . . .** and **I don't like . . .** by asking the children which fruits they like and dislike.
- ◉ You might like to extend this and do a class survey of the children's likes and dislikes.
- Play a Yes/No game. Put a list of words which take **a** or **an** on the board. Ask a child to choose one of the words. The others try to guess what it is, asking only questions that can be answered by Yes or No.
- ◉ Do a role play. Firstly, demonstrate it yourself using one of the children. Put the children in pairs. Make one child a shopkeeper and the other a customer. Get them to practise saying: *An apple, please* or *I would like an orange*. This will obviously work best if you bring in items for the children to buy and sell. If you bring eggs, hard-boil them first!
- ◉ Play a miming game. Give the children pieces of paper with words written on them (or whisper to the child), e.g. *a book, an umbrella, an apple*. Children mime according to what you've given them. The rest of the class tries to guess.

Parents

- Using pages 8–9, play a game of I Spy with your child, e.g. *I spy with my little eye something beginning with **a*** (an apple). Try to make sure that your child puts the right article in front of the noun.
- Go into your kitchen. Put several objects on the table, e.g. an egg, an orange, a book, a bottle, an apple. Tell your child to look at these things for one minute. Now cover all the objects with a cloth. See how many things your child can remember.
- Put several different objects into a bag. Ask your child to put his hand in the bag and feel the objects. He should try to guess what the objects are and say their names in English, using **a** or **an**.
- Play a game of shops. Put a number of objects to buy and sell on a table. Pretend to be the shopkeeper. Encourage your child to ask for things using *I'd like . . .* Take turns to be the customer and the shopkeeper.
- Write out the names of fruits, vegetables and other objects on pieces of paper. Put the same objects on a table and ask your child to match up the words and objects.
- Play a game of Hangman. Use a variety of words which take **a** and **an**. Take turns to play the game.
- When you cook a meal, ask your child to tell you what ingredients you are using, in English.
- Choose a variety of objects around the house. Make a list of them and write each one on a separate piece of paper. Send your child on a hunt for the objects. He should put the correct piece of paper beside each object.

Chapter 3 Adjectives

Words

bad	good	red	tall
beetle	gorilla	sad	thin
big	green	short	wheelchair
blue	happy	sky	yellow
fat	little	sun	young
flamingo	old		

Questions to ask children

Pages 12–13

- What is going on in this picture? *A football match.*
- Who is playing who? *Monkeys are playing elephants.*
- How many players are in each team?
- Who do you think will win the match?
- Who is supporting the elephants?
- Who is supporting the monkeys?
- How do you know? *They have each got a letter* ***M*** *or* ***E*** *which shows whose side they're on.*
- Do you like football?
- What other sports do you like?

Just for fun

Ask the children to find these things:

An animal with a telescope. A 'To Let' sign.
A squirrel chewing the goal post. A baby bird.
A mole with a pop gun.

Ask the children if they can find Smuff.
He is carving his girlfriend's initials on the tree trunk.

Can they see the red lizard?
He is pulling the elephant goalkeeper's tail.

Pages 14–15

- Do the elephants look happy or sad?
- Do the monkeys look happy or sad?
- Who has won the football match?
- What is the score? *Monkeys 5, Elephants 0.*
- What has happened to Mrs Elephant?
  She fell over on page 12 and is being taken to the doctor's.
- What is the bird giving to the gorilla?

Just for fun

Ask the children to find these things:

A pink rabbit. A crocodile. A blue bird.
A butterfly. A teddy bear.

Can they see the red lizard?
He is pulling the tortoise's tail.

Exercise A

Written. Children circle the words that they find in the puzzle. The words are written horizontally and vertically. The following words are in the puzzle:

BAD	GOOD	THIN
BIG	HAPPY	YELLOW
BLUE	OLD	YOUNG
FAT	RED	
GREEN	SAD	

- Extra: make your own word searches using only colours or other adjectives that your children are familiar with. Ask the children to read aloud the words they have found.

Exercise B

Written. Children fill in the gaps.

1 I'm a fat monkey.
2 I'm a tall monkey.
3 I'm an old monkey.
4 I'm a young monkey.
5 I'm a sad elephant.

- Extra: do the exercise orally using *I'm*. Next, revise *He's* and *She's* so that the children do the exercise by saying, e.g., *He's a happy gorilla.*

Exercise C

Oral or written. Children make as many sentences as they can. They must use a word from each of the columns. Suggested sentences:

Mr Monkey is fat.
The tree is green.
The snake is bad.
An elephant is sad.
The sky is blue.
Mrs Rabbit is happy.

- Extra: divide the class into groups of four. Give four sheets of paper to each group. All children write **A**, or **The** or **Mr** at the top of the sheet, then fold it over and pass it on. Next, each child writes the name of an animal, folds the paper over again and passes it on. Now tell the children to write **is** and pass the paper on. They should all finish by writing an adjective. Finally the children unfold all the papers and take turns to read one out to the whole class.

Exercise D

Written. Children colour in Mrs Elephant according to the colour key provided.

- Extra: if you have access to different colours of chalk, draw the outline of an animal or a large object such as a house on the board. Ask the children to tell you how to colour it in, e.g. *The windows are red. The door is blue.*

Other things to do

Quick activities

- Practise the adjectives using flashcards. Add any extra adjectives you want to teach your children.
- Turn back to pages 12–13. Ask questions about the animals in the picture which are not already covered by the text, e.g. the old tortoise, the big gorilla, the little monkey.
- If you want further practice, choose another page in the book and ask the children to describe the characters (try pages 34–35, for example).
- Draw things on the board. For instance, a fat monkey, a tall boy, a big house, a small book, a big book. Ask the children to guess what you are drawing.
- Divide the board into two columns. Write a list of opposite adjectives in each column, like this:

  young short
  fat bad
  sad old
  tall thin
  big little
  good happy

  Now ask the children to tell you where to draw connecting lines to show which adjective is the opposite of another.

Longer activities

- ⊙ Get the children to mime the adjectives. They could do this in pairs, e.g. *We're happy monkeys. We're sad rabbits.* The class guesses what they are.
- ⊙ Divide the children into two teams, or into small groups. Give each group a list of things they must find, e.g. *a red pencil, a big book, a small piece of paper, a thin notebook, a green pencil case.* Allow the groups or teams five minutes to find all the things and return to their desks. The first team to find all the right things wins the game.
- ⊙ Play Chinese Whispers, either with the class as a whole, or in smaller groups. Sit the children in a line. Whisper a sentence like *Mr Lion is fat and happy* to the first child. Tell him to whisper it to the next child and so on. The last child in the line shouts out what he's heard. (It is usually wrong, but it's fun!)
- ⊙ Give each child a piece of paper on which you have written a noun and an adjective, e.g. *a happy cat.* One by one children draw these on the blackboard. The class guesses what the picture is.
- Play an 'In the Jungle' game, this time adding adjectives, e.g. *In the jungle I see a fat monkey.* Next child: *In the jungle I see a tall, fat monkey* etc.
- If you want to vary this game, bring in a ball. Children throw the ball to one another. Whoever has the ball has to add an adjective.
- ⊙ Divide the children into groups. Give each group an adjective and a sheet of paper. (Each sheet should be the same size.) Ask each group to draw a picture which illustrates the adjective they have been given. When they have finished, label each drawing in big letters with the relevant adjective. Display the drawings in a line along the classroom wall.

Parents

- Take turns with your child to mime some of the adjectives in this chapter, e.g. *happy, sad, young, old.*
- Hide several objects in a room in your house, e.g. *a blue T-shirt, an old newspaper, a photograph of your child as a baby, a green cup.* Write a list of the objects on a piece of paper. Give it to your child and tell him which room to go to. Give him five minutes to find the objects.
- Cut pictures out of magazines or newspapers, e.g. *an old man, a young girl, a big building, a small dog.* Your child labels each picture with the correct adjective.
- If you have a garden, send your child (and a friend, if possible) on a treasure hunt. Tell him to find several objects, e.g. *a long stick, a green leaf, a small stone.*
- Watch a television programme together. Encourage him to describe the people or animals using the adjectives he has learnt, in English, e.g. *She's a happy girl. He's a fat mouse. He's a tall man.*
- Write the adjectives in the chapter (adding some if you wish) on separate pieces of paper. Write the equivalent words in your own language on pieces of paper. See if your child can match the English words with yours.
- Look at some other pages in the book (34–35 or 38–39, for example). Help your child to describe the animals using the adjectives he has learnt. You can revise colours with your child using any page in the book.
- Play a game of opposites. Say an adjective, e.g. *happy.* Your child should try to say the opposite word: *sad.* Take turns to think of an adjective.
- Draw the outline of a big imaginary animal. Draw lines across it to separate it into seven parts. Number each part 1–7. Give your child a colour list, e.g. *1 = red, 5 = blue.* Tell him to colour in the animal according to the numbers.

BOOK 1

Chapter 4 There is and There are

Words

blackboard	mountain	river
coconut	picture	teacher
guitar	plant	telephone
letterbox	pupil	toy

Questions to ask children

Pages 16–17

- Where are the animals? *At school.*
- Who is the teacher?
- How many pupils are there?
- Are they good pupils or bad pupils?
- What lesson are they doing?
- Is the sum on the board right?
- Can you see some books?
- Who is throwing a paper aeroplane? *The crocodile.*
- What else can you see?

Just for fun

Ask the children to find these things:

Rabbits playing cards.
A worm in an apple.
A frog.
Eyes in the bookcase.
A hand coming out of the tree.
A monkey picking a banana.

Can they see the red lizard?
He's spraying the letters Q and S on the teacher's desk. They stand for Quite Soon, because he's hoping that the lesson will end quite soon.

Pages 18–19

- What are the animals sitting on the branch doing?
- What are the crocodiles doing?
- What is the gorilla painting?
- What are the pupils doing?
- What is the teacher doing?
- Who is posting a letter?
- Can you see a mouse?
- Are there seven red flowers on page 19?
- Are there five books on the teacher's desk?

Just for fun

Ask the children to find these things:

Mushrooms or toadstools.
A monkey hiding in a bush.
A blue and pink butterfly.
A ladybird.

Can they see the red lizard?
He's tickling a monkey with a feather.

Exercise A

Written. Children fill in the gaps.

There is . . .	There are . . .
1 a giraffe	6 six rabbits
2 a frog	7 five crocodiles
3 a tortoise	8 two snakes
4 a gorilla	9 two butterflies
5 a television	10 four monkeys

- Extra: do the exercise by dividing the class into two or four teams. The first team to get the answers correct wins.

Exercise B

Oral or written. Children write down the other things they can see in the picture. Suggested answers:

There are seven books. There is a football. There is a pen. There are three mountains. There is a mouse.

- Extra: play a memory game. Divide the children into small groups. Give them a few minutes to study the picture. Tell them to close their books and write down or say all that they can remember.

Exercise C

Oral or written. Children answer the question with *Yes, there is* or *No, there isn't.*

1 Is there a football?	*Yes, there is.*
2 Is there a chair?	*Yes, there is.*
3 Is there a pencil?	*No, there isn't.*
4 Is there a coconut?	*No, there isn't.*
5 Is there a river?	*No, there isn't.*

- Extra: ask similar questions about the room you are in.

Exercise D

Oral or written. Children answer the question with *Yes, there are* or *No, there aren't.*

1 Are there three mountains?	*Yes, there are.*
2 Are there eight birds?	*No, there aren't.*
3 Are there six crocodiles?	*No, there aren't.*
4 Are there three snakes?	*No, there aren't.*
5 Are there five bananas?	*No, there aren't.*

- Extra: play a True or False game. Make up some true and some false statements about the chapter, e.g. *There are ten birds on pages 16–17.* (False.)

Other things to do

Quick activities

- Try playing a game of I Spy: *I spy with my little eye something beginning with* ***d***. (desk)
- Revise numbers and the vocabulary learnt by asking the children about their own classroom, e.g. *What is in your classroom? What subjects do you study? How many pupils are there? How many desks are there?*
- You can do this with other pages in the book, e.g. *How many monkeys are there on pages 12–13? How many frogs on page 22? How many birds on page 23?*
- Play a True or False game. Write out a number of questions about the two pictures. Organize the children into teams. The first team to complete all the questions wins.
- ◉ As a variation, stand the children in a line. If a statement is true they should jump to the right, if it is false, they jump to the left. If too slow or wrong, the child is out. The last one standing in line is the winner.
- ◉ Arrange a role-play. Divide the children into groups and let them organize their own class. Give them a couple of minutes and then get them to swap roles, so that they all have a go at being the teacher.
- Let the children tell you what to draw on the board. Refuse to draw anything unless they say, for example, *There is an apple. There are two birds.*
- ◉ Bring in up to ten small buttons, dried beans or coins. Put your hands behind your back and put some of the beans or coins in each hand. Ask the children to guess how many you've got in each hand. They should guess by saying *There are four . . .* Let the children have a turn at holding the beans.

Longer activities

- Do a picture dictation. Give each child a piece of paper. Slowly say *In my picture there is a tree. In my picture there is a house. In my picture there is a flower* etc. Gradually introduce the plural, e.g. *In my picture there are two monkeys.* Children draw the things that you say.
- ◉ Extend this by going round the class giving each child the opportunity to add an object to the picture. Child 1: *In my picture there is a cat.* Child 2: *In my picture there is an apple.* The rest of the class draws.
- ◉ Choose a location with your children, e.g. *a desert island* or *an undiscovered planet*. Write a number of sentences on the board, e.g. *There is a river. There are two tall mountains. There is a castle.* Put the children into teams. Each team draws a picture of the chosen location.
- ◉ Turn this into a bigger project by giving each team separate pieces of paper and specific things to draw. When all the teams have finished their drawings, stick them all together to make a poster of the planet or island you have chosen. You can label each of the items drawn with **There is** and **There are** as a reminder.
- ◉ Put the children into pairs. Tell them to draw a box each. In the box they should put any number from one to ten of the following: apples, pencils, books. They must not show their box to their partner. The children take turns to guess what is in each other's box using **There is** and **There are**.

Parents

- Choose a room in your house and go into it with your child. Take turns to describe what is in the room, using **there is** and **there are**, like this: *There is a television. There are two chairs. There is a bed* etc.
- Extend this by running to touch the object described. Score one point for each correctly identified object.
- Get a large sheet of paper. Tell your child that you are both going to draw a magical island. Take turns to say what should be on the island, e.g. Child: *On the island there is a castle.* (Parent draws castle.) Parent: *On the island there are two mountains.* (Child draws two mountains.)
- Put some sweets or other small objects in your hands and put your hands behind your back. Encourage your child to guess how many sweets you have in your right hand and then in your left hand. Take turns to play the game.
- Send your child (and a friend if possible) into your garden or a room in the house. Give them a list of things to find, e.g. *Find three red things. Find a small thing.* The child should write down or say what he has found, like this: *There are three red flowers. There is a snail.*
- Using the book, devise a mini quiz. Write a list of sentences like these: *On page 28 there are five* ______ . *On page 12 there is a grey* ______ . *There are* ______ *hats on page 29. There are* ______ *monkeys on page 14.* Your child looks through the book and fills in the gaps you have left.

Chapter 5 Imperatives

Words

bear	hand	open	smile
clap	head	opposite	stand
dance	jump	read	toe
door	laugh	sit	touch
eat	lie down	sleep	

Questions to ask children

Pages 20–21

- What is happening? *The young jungle animals are having a fitness training session.*
- Who is training them? *The tiger.*
- Are the baby elephants tired?
- Who is jumping?
- Who is running?
- Who is smiling?
- Who is sleeping?
- Should the bears be sleeping?

Practise some more negative imperatives.

Just for fun

Ask the children to find the following things:

A bird in a plant.
A snake and a caterpillar in the tree.
The bird (flamingo) refusing to stand up.
A fly above a crocodile's nose.

Can they see the red lizard?
He's on a branch trying to cut the tortoise's swinging vine.

Pages 22–23

- Where are the animals? *In a tree house.*
- Who do you think lives in the house?
- Where's Mr Tiger?
- How many blue birds are there?
- How many doors are there in the tree house?
- Would you like to live in a tree house?

Just for fun

Ask the children to find the following things:

A sign on a door.	Two books.
An animal asleep.	A fish.

Can they see the red lizard?
He's tickling the rhinoceros's nose with a feather.

Exercise A

Written. Children fill in the gaps. Could also be done orally.

1 Lie down.
2 Stand up.
3 Sit.
4 Jump.
5 Sleep.

- Extra: put children into pairs. Tell one of them to be the frog and the other the tortoise. The frog must obey the tortoise. When they have practised the imperatives in Exercise A, they swap roles.

Exercise B

Physical. Children read the commands and act them out.

- Extra: get the children to mime the actions. The class guesses what the action is.

Exercise C

Oral or written. Children to find the opposite command to the one written down. They can draw connecting lines in their books.

Run! *Mr Rabbit*	Laugh! *Mr Bird*
Dance! *Mr Monkey*	Sleep! *Mr Rhino*
Read! *Mr Owl*	Eat! *Mr Bull*

- Extra: turn back to pages 20–21. Ask the children to say the opposite of each of Mr Tiger's orders.

Other things to do

Quick activities

- Demonstrate each of the new verbs using mime. Get the children to copy you until they are all familiar with the new words.
- Go through the parts of the body with the children. Draw a person on the board and ask the children to help you label the parts of the body.
- Let the children give you orders. Go round the class allowing each child to give you one order, e.g. *Go to the door. Stand up. Open a book.*
- Ask for two volunteers and get them to sit either side of you. As you say each action, do it and get them to follow you. Then repeat, getting them to do it on their own. Finally get the whole class to join in. Once they are familiar with all the actions, you could play Mr Tiger Says: a variation of Simon Says. Let the children have a go at being Mr Tiger.
- Put all the new verbs on the board in one column. Now put the negative imperatives in another column, but in a different order from that used in the first column. Ask the children to tell you which are the opposites. Draw lines between the columns to match them up.

Longer activities

- To extend this last exercise and make it more energetic, clear a space in the room. Before the lesson starts, write imperatives in positive and negative forms on separate pieces of paper. Stick all the positive imperatives on a wall on one side of the room and all the negatives on the other side. Give the children five minutes to move the pieces of paper so that they form pairs of positive and negative imperatives.
- Do a picture dictation with the children. Give them each a sheet of paper. Slowly read out what they should draw, like this: *Draw a head. Draw two eyes. Draw a big nose.*
- Put the children into small groups. Give each group a large sheet of paper. Ask them to draw the silliest person they can think of. Encourage them to give their person as many parts of the body as they like, e.g. *two heads, ten eyes, three arms*. When each group has finished, swap all the drawings round. Ask each group

Parents

- Check that your child knows all the parts of the body. Draw a stick man on a large sheet of paper and label the parts of the body with your child.
- Help your child to draw a monster. Slowly tell him what to draw, like this: *draw a head, draw five eyes, draw a small nose, draw six ears . . .*
- Do various actions, e.g. touch your head, open a newspaper, shut a door. Get your child to say what you are doing.
- If you know the song *'Head and shoulders, knees and toes'*, sing it with your child and do the actions at the same time.
- Write the verbs in the positive and negative forms on separate pieces of card, e.g. *run, don't run, laugh, don't laugh* (four pieces of card). Play a game of opposites with your child. Encourage him to match up the cards.
- Play the same game orally when you feel that your child is confident with the new words. You say, e.g., *don't smile*, your child says *smile*.
- If you have made cards, you can play a game of Snap with your child.
- Let your child give you orders which you obey, e.g. *stand up, sit down, go to the door*. Take turns to play the game.
- Play a game of Mr Tiger Says with your child. If he has brothers or sisters, encourage them to join in. The more people play, the more fun it is.

Chapter 6 This is or That is?

Words

boat
carrot
dress
fish
flower
hat
house
shoe
snail
sun

Questions to ask children

Pages 26–27

- Where are the animals?
- Who is driving the boat?
- Who is fishing?
- Is it a big fish or a small fish?
- Is it a hot day?
- How do you know?
- Is the sun near or far?
- Is the mountain near or far?
- What else is far away?

Just for fun

Ask the children to find the following things:

Green eyes in the leaves.
A snail wearing a tie.
A face in the porthole on the boat.
A baby frog relaxing on a leaf.

Can they see the red lizard?
He's on a leaf throwing a worm in the air.

Pages 28–29

- Are the animals on the river now?
- Where are they?
- How many monkeys can you see?
- Is there a television?
- Who is watching it?
- Can you see a monkey sleeping?
- What has the yellow owl got?
- Is it close to him or far from him?
- What is the green owl pointing at?
- Is it close to him or far from him?

Just for fun

Ask the children to find the following things:

A spider's web.
A sock.
Three butterflies.
A bat.
A monkey sleeping.
A purple flower.

Can they see the red lizard?
He's sawing through the tree.

Exercise A

Written. Children fill in the gaps. Could also be done orally.

1 That is an owl.
2 This is a banana.
3 That is a snake.
4 This is a flower.
5 This is a shoe.
6 That is a rabbit.
7 That is a butterfly.
8 This is a carrot.
9 That is a dress.
10 This is a hat.

- Extra: Write a list of things in the classroom on the board. Put the children into groups. Tell them to write a list of five things that are close to where they are sitting using **This is . . .** and five things that are far from where they are sitting using **That is . . .**

Other things to do

Quick activities

- Take the children outside, if this is possible. Point at various things around you that are nearby, e.g. a swing, a dustbin, a tree. Ask the children questions, e.g. *What's this?* The children reply according to what you are pointing at.
- When the children are used to the question: *What's this?* ask them to show you some things that are far from where you are standing, e.g. a road in the distance, a car, someone walking down the street, the sun, a cloud. Say to the children: *What's that?* or *Who's that?* Try to emphasize that we use **that** for more distant people and things.
- Once you are confident that the children have understood the difference between **this** and **that**, mix your questions. Point, for example, at something nearby – a child, perhaps – and ask: *Who's this?* Then point at something that is far away and ask: *What's that?*
- Pretend that you have lost your memory. Go round the classroom pointing at objects which the children are familiar with. For example, point at the board and look perplexed. Say to the children: *What's this?* They should answer you by saying: *It's the board*. Now go right up to the door and peer at it. Say: *What's this?* Approach one of the children as if you had never set eyes on them before and ask: *Who's this?* Let the children answer you each time.
- Cut some pictures of objects out of old magazines. Stick them all at random onto a large piece of card to make a collage. Put it up on the classroom wall. Point at individual objects and ask: *What's this?* or *Is this a house?* The children should answer, correcting you where necessary.

- Ask the children to turn back to pages 26–27. Point at various things in the picture and make a wrong statement about them, e.g. point at the flamingo in the sky and say: *That's an elephant*. Let the children correct you.

Longer activities

- Introduce some new vocabulary, either using flashcards or real examples. Teach the children the words for various items of clothing, e.g. hat, shoe, skirt, shirt, jumper, trousers, sock etc.
- Extend this by either bringing in real examples of clothing, or by cutting pictures of individual items of clothing out of magazines. If you have real examples, hold each one up in turn and say, for example, *Is this a skirt?* The children tell you whether it is or not. If it's not, they should point at the thing and say: *No, that's a shoe*. If you are using pictures, stick them on to a sheet of paper and do the exercise in the same way.
- Play a game, preferably outside if that is possible. Tell the children that every time you say a sentence with **that**, they must run away from you. If you say a sentence with **this**, they should run towards you. Line the children up in front of you a reasonable distance away. Now say, e.g. *That's a tiger!* The children should all run away from you. Then say, e.g., *This is a nice classroom*. The children should run towards you. Once they are confident, try to catch them out by saying something irrelevant, such as: *What a lovely day!* Anyone who moves is out.
- ◉ Ask one of the children to pretend that he has just arrived from another planet. Tell him to go round the classroom asking the other children questions with *What's this? What's that?* and *Who's this? Who's that?* Give the children each a turn at being the alien.
- ◉ Blindfold one child. Divide the rest of the class into two groups. One group stands as far away from the blindfolded child as possible, the other group stands quite close to him. Tell the children in the far group that they must all make roaring noises like a lion. The near group makes squeaking noises like a mouse. When you clap your hands all the children must be silent. The blindfolded child can choose either to say: *Who's that? Roar, lion, roar!* or *Who's this? Squeak, mouse, squeak!* You then point at one of the children. The child in question either roars or squeaks according to whether he is in the near or far group. The blindfolded child must try to guess who the child is. If he succeeds, the squeaker or roarer becomes the next blindfolded child.

Parents

- Turn to pages 26–27. Point at various things in the picture, e.g. the sun, the houses on the riverbank, the bird in the sky. Ask your child whether he thinks these things are near or far from the animals. Try to make sure that he understands that we use **this** for things that are close to us and **that** for things that are far away.
- Say some sentences in your own language, e.g. *That's the moon. That's a star. This is the television. This is your brother*. Ask your child to translate them into English to check that he understands the concept.
- Play a game together. Take turns to say sentences using **this** and **that**. Play the game like this: (You) *This is an apple*. (Child) *That is the door*.
- Pretend that you don't know where you are any more. You might be a creature from another planet, for example. Ask your child to guide you round the house telling you what things are. Ask your child questions and try to look surprised. Look at the cooker, for instance, and ask: *What's this?* Your child answers by saying: *This is a cooker*. If you have a cat or dog, try to look horrified and say: *What's this?* (or *What's that?* if it is in the garden, or some distance away). When you see another member of your family, look terrified and say to your child: *Who's this?* It will amuse your child to see you behaving in such a peculiar way and help him to remember the difference between **this** and **that**.

BOOK 1 **Chapter 7** **Who** or **What?**

Words

buffalo, drink, tourist, who, cherry, pear, what

Questions to ask children

Pages 30–31

- Which animals haven't we seen before?
- Why are they asking lots of questions? *They haven't been to this bit of the jungle before: they are tourists.*
- If you could go anywhere in the world, where would you go?
- Can you see any animals with cameras?
- Can you see any animals with sunglasses?
- Who is leading the tourists through the jungle? *Mr Lion.*
- Who is dropping a coconut?
- Who is it going to land on?

Just for fun

Ask the children to find these things:

A crocodile wearing a bracelet.
A furry purple tourist.
A blue bird.
A purple hat.

Can they see the red lizard?
He's pointing a bow and arrow at Mrs Giraffe.

Pages 32–33

- What is happening in this picture? *The animals are having a fancy dress party.*
- Who is playing the music for the party?
- What are the animals at the top of these pages doing? *They are dancing.*
- What are the young animals at the bottom of page 32 doing? *Drinking fruit juices.*
- Who is serving the fruit juices?
- Where else in the book can you see the mole? *Page 12, on the football pitch.*

Just for fun

Ask the children to find these things:

Three animals wearing sunglasses.
A blue butterfly.
An animal dressed as a house.
A guitar.

Can they see the red lizard?
He's playing with the baby elephant's chair.

Exercise A

Oral or written. Children fill in the gaps.

1 Mr Buffalo.
2 Mr Snake.
3 Mrs Lion.
4 Mr Lion.
5 Mr Crocodile.
6 Mrs Giraffe.
7 Mrs Elephant.

◉ Extra: play a game of Blind Man's Buff. Blindfold one child and see if he can guess the names of other children by touch alone. Remind the children not to speak.

Exercise B

Oral or written. Children fill in the gaps.

What's this? (Six times.)

◉ Extra: put the children in pairs. Check that they know the names of the fruits shown on the animals' bottles of fruit juice. Tell them to take turns to ask and answer the questions, e.g. *What's this? It's a pineapple drink.*

Exercise C

Oral or written. Children fill in the gaps.

1 What is this?
2 Who is this?
3 Who is this?
4 What is this?

- Extra: turn to other pages in the book, e.g. pages 16–17. Point at the characters and ask: *Who's this?*, then point at the telephone, the guitar, a desk, the plant, the apple and ask: *What's this?*

Other things to do

Quick activities

- Pretend that you have never been in the classroom before. Point at things and ask: *What's this?* The children answer your questions.
- ⊙ Extend this by asking each child to go round the classroom saying: *What's this?* The rest of the class shouts out the answers, e.g. *It's a desk. It's a blackboard.*
- ⊙ When they are confident with **what?** tell them to ask **who?** questions as well. If you are able to take the children outside, do the same in the playground.
- Bring in pictures of well-known people and objects which your children will know the names of. Use them as flashcards, saying *Who's this?* and *What's this?* as appropriate. The children answer your questions.
- Then drill the children to say **who?** and **what?** as you hold up the appropriate picture.
- ⊙ Give each child a slip of paper with the name of an animal that makes a noise written on it, e.g. *Mr Lion, Mr Dog, Mrs Cat.* Tell the children to make the noise that their animal makes. The rest of the class guesses who they are.
- ⊙ Bring in a ball and a cassette recorder. Sit the children in a circle on the floor. Tell them to throw or pass the ball round. While they are doing this play some music on the cassette player. Every so often, stop the music and ask: *Who's got the ball?* The children call out the name of the child with the ball.
- ⊙ If you think your children are confident enough with **what?**, ask them to mime a variety of activities, e.g. swimming, eating, sleeping. Ask: *What is he doing?* The class tries to guess what is being mimed.

Longer activities

- Draw a picture on the board making only one line at a time. The children try to guess what you are drawing before you draw the next bit.
- Ask the children a series of questions about pages 32–33 with **who?**, e.g. *Who is drinking a banana drink? Who is dressed in white?* Don't forget that you could use other pages in the book for the same purpose: try pages 28–29, for example.
- ⊙ Give each child the name of a person or an object that the whole class will know. Play a Yes/No game. The class tries to guess what or who the child is by asking only questions that can be answered by Yes or No.
- ⊙ Divide the children into pairs or small groups. Ask them all to draw an object. When they have finished, swap all their drawings round. The children try to guess what each object is.
- Bring in a set of everyday household objects. Put them in a bag, one at a time, without the children seeing. Let each child feel the object and try to guess what it is.
- Play a guessing game. Choose several pictures of things the children will be familiar with, e.g. a toothbrush, a fork, a television, a football. Now cut a section out of each picture. The children try to guess what the picture is of by looking at the section only.
- ⊙ Ask the children to bring in a photograph of themselves when they were younger. Mix all the photographs up. Hand one to each child and let them try to guess who is who.

Parents

- Look at other pages in the book, for example, 8–9, 16–17, 38–39. Practise identifying the difference between objects and people (or in this case animals), by asking questions with **who?** and **what?**
- Cut out a selection of pictures of objects and people from magazines. Test your child by getting him to say **who?** or **what?** according to whether the picture he is looking at is of a person or an object.
- Look at a family photograph album together. Ask *Who's this?* and let your child answer.
- Find some pictures of well-known objects, e.g. a saucepan, a house, a postbox. Cut a piece out of each picture and show it to your child. Ask him to try to guess what the object is.
- Make noises, e.g. the noise of an animal or a car or a musical instrument. Ask: *What am I?* Get your child to guess what you are pretending to be each time you make a noise. Take turns to play the game.
- Take turns to draw familiar objects on a sheet of paper, e.g. a door, a table, a cat, a book. You each try to guess what the other has drawn.
- Blindfold your child. Hand him objects one by one, e.g. a book, an orange, an egg, a shirt. He must try to identify each object by touch alone. Let him choose some objects for you to identify, too.
- Make up a list of questions, e.g. *Who delivers letters? Who teaches you at school? Who drives a car? Who cooks supper?* Let your child answer each question.
- Play the same game, using **what?** questions, e.g. *What has four legs? What do you sleep in? What do you write with?*
- Tell your child that you are going to invent a story about a secret castle together. Ask your child questions with **what?** and **who?**, e.g. *What colour is the castle? What is it made of? Who lives in the castle? What does the person do? What does he eat?*

Chapter 8 **In**, **on**, **under** and **next to**

Words

bath	house	paw
branch	in	room
caterpillar	leaf	tree trunk
glass	next to	under
hippo	on	

Questions to ask children

Pages 34–35

- Can you point at the monkeys' house?
- Who is riding on the elephant's back?
- Who is sitting in a box of carrots?
- Where does Mr Crocodile live?
- What is he wearing?
- Can you see two animals talking?
- What is Mr Monkey doing? *Surfing.*
- Does he look frightened?
- What is on the hippo's head?

Just for fun

Ask the children to find these things:

A snake in a trumpet/horn.
Someone trying to steal a banana.
A fish biting the lion's tail.
Two insects.

Can they see the red lizard?
He's sawing through a branch by the two houses.

Pages 36–37

- What can you see in the picture?
- Who do you think lives in the room in the tree?
- Can you see a baby elephant?
- How many rabbits can you see?
- Where are they?
- Can you see a bed?
- Where is it?

Just for fun

Ask the children to find the following things:

Two animals playing a game.
Two snakes.
A red flower.
A heart-shaped chair.

Can they see the red lizard?
He's firing his catapult in the air.

Exercise A

Written. Children fill in the gaps. Could also be done orally.

1 The caterpillar is on the leaf.
2 The frog is under the leaf.
3 The rabbit is on the tree trunk.
4 The snake is next to the rabbit.
5 The mouse is in the glass.

- Extra: turn back to pages 34–35. Ask questions about animals not already covered by the text, e.g. the kangaroo and the bear, the rabbit in the box of carrots, the monkey on the elephant's back.

Exercise B

Oral or written. Children describe what they can see in their room.

- Ask the children to draw a picture. Slowly give them instructions. For example: *Draw a bed. Draw a table. Draw a cat under the table. Draw a teddy bear on the bed.*

Exercise C

Written. Children read the text, find the animal described and colour it in.

Exercise D

Oral or written. Children look at Mrs Tortoise's room and describe what they can see. Suggested answers:

A television on the table. A cup next to the television. A teddy bear on the bed. A skateboard under the bed. A carpet/rug on the floor. A picture on the wall. A chair next to the bed.

- Extra: ask the children to imagine what another character's room might be like: Mr Elephant's room, for example. Encourage the children to tell you not only what he would have in his room but also where he would keep his things.

Other things to do

Quick activities

- Turn to pages 8–9. Ask questions with **where?** about the animals in the picture. You can do this with most pages in the book if you need further practice.
- Play a memory game using pages 8–9. Give the children a minute or so to look at the pages. Tell them to close their books. Ask questions with **where?** Either do this with the class as a whole, or make it more competitive by putting the children into teams.
- Stand or sit in various places round the classroom, e.g. stand next to one of the children, get under your desk, stand on a chair. Ask the children to tell you what you're doing, using **on**, **under** and **next to**. You may feel a bit silly, but it will amuse the children and help them to remember the meaning of the prepositions.
- Bring in a teddy bear, or a small toy such as a car. Put it in various positions and ask the children to tell you where it is.
- Tell the children to pick up a pencil or a book. Now ask them to put it, e.g. under a chair, on the floor, in a pencil case, next to a desk.
- Play a True or False game. Prepare statements about one of the pictures in this chapter, or choose another. Suggested questions (pages 36–37): *The rabbit is next to the elephant.* (False.) *The bird is on the branch.* (True.) *The teddy is under the bed.* (False.) *The frog is under the leaf.* (True.)

Longer activities

- Draw the inside of a room on the board. Put in essentials such as a bed, a chair etc. Now ask the children to tell you where to draw other things in the room, e.g. A picture on the wall. A cushion on the chair.
- Do a picture dictation. Slowly tell the children to draw certain things, e.g. *Draw a tree. Draw a cat next to the tree. Draw a flower under the tree.*
- ◉ Devise a treasure hunt. Before the lesson starts, hide small things such as sweets or toys round the classroom. Divide the children into teams. Write a list of clues for each team on the board, e.g. *There is treasure in a cupboard. There is treasure under a book. There is treasure next to the door.* Now tell the children to look for their treasure. If you are able to do this outside in the playground, it would be even better.
- ◉ Divide the children into small groups. Give each group several sheets of paper. Ask them to draw things, e.g. Group 1 draws four tables. Group 2 draws two beds and two chairs. Group 3 draws a television and three pictures. Now ask all the children to draw any object or animal they like. Once all the drawings are finished, cut them out. Take a very large sheet of paper. Get the children to help you decide where to stick each item.

  Once the poster is finished, label it like this: *There is a cat on the bed. There is a picture on the wall. There are shoes under the table. There is a chair next to the bed.*
- ◉ Tell the children that during the night Smuff arrived to visit the school. Unfortunately you have lost him. You know that he is hiding somewhere in the classroom, but you haven't yet been able to find him. Ask the children to tell you where to look for him. Go to each place as they call out their suggestions, e.g. *Is he in the cupboard? No, he's not. Is he under the desk?*
- Play a variation of Simon Says with the children. Say, for example: *Mr Tiger says put your hand in your pocket. Mr Tiger says put both hands on your head. Mr Tiger says get under your desks. Mr Tiger says sit on a chair.*

Parents

- Check that your child understands the meaning of the prepositions by asking him what the equivalent words are in your own language. Ask a series of questions. Get him to translate them for you, e.g. *The television is on the table. There is water in the glass.*
- Turn to other pages in the book, e.g., 16–17 or 26–27. Ask your child questions with **where?**, e.g. (16–17) *Where can you see a frog?* (On the bookcase.)
- Choose some small everyday objects, e.g. a rubber, a teabag, a button. Put them **in**, **on**, **under** and **next to** things on a table. Now ask your child to tell you where each one is, in English, e.g. *The teabag is under the cup. The button is in the glass* etc.
- Draw a room on a large sheet of paper. Draw a bed, a chair, a table, but do not add any detail. Now ask your child to add things to the picture, e.g. *Draw a teddy bear on the bed. Draw a football next to the chair. Draw a picture on the wall. Draw yourself in the bed.*
- Send your child (and a friend, if possible) on a treasure hunt round the house or garden. Hide some small rewards such as sweets or toys. Give him a list of clues like these: *There is some treasure on a bookcase. There is something in the cupboard. There is something under a flower pot. There is some treasure next to the television.*
- Play a game of Mr Tiger Says. Say, for example, *Mr Tiger says get under the table. Mr Tiger says sit on a chair. Mr Tiger says hide in a cupboard.* Take turns to play the game with your child. If you can get other members of your family to join in, it'll be even more fun.
- Play a guessing game. Take turns to think of an object in the room, like this: (Parent thinks of a book on the sofa.) Decide beforehand which preposition you are going to use. Your child asks you questions, e.g. *Is it on the table?* (No.) *Is it on the floor?* (No.) *Is it on the sofa?* (Yes.) *Is it a book?* (Yes.) When your child is confident with each preposition, you can keep the preposition secret, too. For example, *Is it next to the television?* (No.) *Is it under the table?* (No.) *Is it in the cupboard?* (Yes.)

BOOK 1 Chapter 9 Has got and have got

Words

body	have got	nice	stripes
camera	ice cream	nose	sunglasses
car	leg	paintbrush	tail
clothes	long	sharp	teeth
ear	neck	skin	tooth
eye	necklace	spots	towel
has got	newspaper	starfish	wing

Questions to ask children

Pages 38–39

- What are the animals doing?
- What sort of party is it?
- Is it a birthday party?
- Is it a wedding?
- How many animals have got presents?
- Is there a cake?
- Do you like parties?
- What did you get for your last birthday?
- What is Mrs Crocodile going to do with her ice cream? *Throw it at Mr Crocodile.*

Just for fun

Ask the children to find the following things:

An ear-ring.
Nine hats.
A mouse on the crocodile's tail.
A rabbit wearing a hat.

Can they see the red lizard?
No, this is the page he's not on.

Pages 40–41

- What are the animals doing now? *They're painting.*
- Who is painting Mr Crocodile?
- Is Mr Crocodile happy?
- What is the monkey on page 41 painting?
- What is the bird (flamingo) on page 41 painting?
- How many monkeys are there?
- How many birds are there?

Just for fun

Ask the children to find these things:

A paint splash on Mr Crocodile's tail.
Someone stealing some ice cream.
A mouse in a paint pot.
A newspaper.

Can they see the red lizard?
He's squeezing paint onto a rabbit.

Exercise A

Oral or written. Children say what each animal has got.

1 The bird has got four paint brushes.
2 The snake has got a pencil.
3 The frog has got a pen.
4 The owl has got a newspaper.
5 The bird (parrot) has got a camera.
6 The bear has got a book.
7 The lizard has got an ice cream.

- Extra: ask the children to open their books at pages 8–9. Tell them to look at the picture for two minutes. Now tell them to shut the book. Ask them questions, e.g. *Who has got an orange? Who has got some eggs?*

Exercise B

Oral or written. Children describe Mr Crocodile, using the words listed.

He's got small blue eyes.
He's got green skin.
He's got a long nose.
He's got sharp teeth.
He's got short legs.
He's got a long tail.
He's got nice clothes.

- Extra: turn back to pages 38–39. Ask the children to describe either Mr or Mrs Elephant in the same way.

Exercise C

Colouring. Children colour in the two birds according to the descriptions given.

- Extra: draw an animal or a person on the board. Get the children to direct your drawing, using **has got**, e.g. *He's got a blue jacket. He's got big eyes.*

Exercise D

Oral or written. Children look at the two pictures and describe the changes. Let the children circle the differences in their books and then help them to describe what has changed. If you have chosen to teach them the negative of has/have got, encourage them to use it.
Suggested answers:

Picture 1 has got birds.
Picture 2 hasn't got birds.
The tortoise hasn't got a book.
The tortoise has got a book.
Picture 1 has got a starfish.
Picture 2 hasn't got a starfish.
The tortoise hasn't got sunglasses.
The tortoise has got sunglasses.
The umbrella has got spots.
The umbrella hasn't got spots.
The towel has got spots.
The towel hasn't got spots.

- Extra: make your own Spot the Difference drawings. Divide the children into pairs and ask them to compare the drawings you have given them.

Other things to do

Quick activities

- Ask each child to say one thing about his appearance, including his clothing. Start it off yourself by saying, e.g., *I've got a blue shirt.*
- Ask the children to describe one another, like this: *Richard's got short hair. Katya's got brown eyes.* If you are feeling brave, ask the children to describe you. Write their descriptions on the board.
- Divide the children into pairs. Tell them to swap schoolbags. Ask them to empty out each other's schoolbags and make lists of their contents, e.g. *He's got three books. He's got an apple. He's got three pencils.*
- Ask the children to think about their toys at home. Go round the class asking each child to say one thing he's got. Child 1: *I've got a train set.* Child 2: *I've got a teddy bear.*
- Using pages 38–39, make a list of true and false statements. Either write them on the board, or read them to the children. They tell you whether they are true or false, e.g. *Mrs Giraffe's got a short neck.* (False.) *Mr Elephant's got a yellow hat.* (True.) Don't forget that if you need further practice, you can do this with most pages in the book.
- Play a chain game with the children. Ask them to imagine a fantastical animal. They then take turns to say one thing each about the animal, e.g. Child 1: *He's got pink skin.* Child 2: *He's got pink skin and green eyes.* Child 3: *He's got pink skin, green eyes and one tooth.*
- Play a guessing game. Each child thinks of an animal and says a sentence or two about him, e.g. (Mr Crocodile.) *He's got sharp teeth. He's got a long tail.* The class tries to guess which animal is being described.

Longer activities

- Clear a space and ask all the children to stand up. Tell them that you are going to say a number of sentences about a person. If they fit the description in any way, they are out of the game. Mix your sentences so that someone isn't out every time. Play the game like this: (You) *You've got a green T-shirt.* The children check to see if they are wearing a green T-shirt. If so, they are out. (You) *You've got red eyes.* No one is out. (You) *You've got blue eyes.* Several children are out. The last person remaining at the end of the game is the winner.
- Give each child a piece of paper on which you've written an object, e.g. an umbrella, a television, an apple. The children take turns to mime having the object on their piece of paper. For instance the child who's got 'an apple' mimes eating an apple. The class tries to guess what he's got.
- Divide the children into small groups. Tell them that they are going to design their ideal house. Give each group a large sheet of paper. Ask them to draw all the things they would most like their ideal house to have, e.g. a swimming pool, a helicopter, hundreds of toys, a chocolate-producing tree in the garden. When they have all finished, ask them to describe the house to the class using **has got**.
- You could turn this into a bigger project by asking the children to write their descriptions next to the objects they have drawn. Display the drawings on the classroom wall.
- Draw a big circle or oblong shape on a large piece of paper. Tell the children that the shape is the beginning of a creature from another planet. Pass the paper round the class. As each child gets it, he must draw one part of the creature and say what it is, for example the first child might draw three legs. He should say: *It's got three legs.* The paper is then passed to the next child. Keep the finished drawing and put it on the wall. Every time you need to remind the children about **has/have got**, point at the creature and ask questions about it, e.g. *How many eyes has it got?*

Parents

- Next time you do the shopping, bring it home and get your child to help you unpack it and put it away. While you are unpacking it, encourage your child to describe each item, using either **I've got** or **We've got**, like this: *I've got a bottle of water. We've got two packets of biscuits.*
- Take a large sheet of paper. Tell your child that you are both going to draw a magical island. Draw the outline of the island, but no other details. Take turns to draw one thing each on the island. Every time you draw something you must say, for example: *The island has got a river. It's got a mountain. It's got a castle.*
- Use pages from the book to describe some of the jungle characters. Point at an animal and ask your child to describe it, e.g. (Mr Lion) *He's got a red jacket. He's got a long tail. He's got big eyes.*
- Or play a guessing game. Choose one of the characters and start to describe him or her, like this: (Mrs Crocodile on page 6) *She's got an orange dress. She's got sharp teeth. She's got green skin.* Your child tries to guess which animal you are describing. Take turns to play the game.
- Ask your child to describe people you both know, e.g. (Mummy) *She's got brown eyes. She's got brown hair.* Do the same while watching a television programme together. Encourage your child to use **has/have got** each time.

BOOK 1 Chapter 10 **Can** for ability

Words

balloon	car	drive	sing
can	climb	fire	spider
can't	cook	guitar	trampoline

Questions to ask children

Pages 42–43

- What is happening in this picture?
- Who is Mr Rhino running after?
- What is Mrs Lion doing?
- Is she good at it?
- What is Mrs Crocodile doing?
- Is she good at it?
- Do you think Mr Elephant is good at jumping?
- Can rabbits jump? Can Smuff jump?
- Who is playing the guitar?
- What kind of animal can sing?
- Do you think birds are good at swimming?

Just for fun

Ask the children to find the following things:

An animal wearing a rubber ring.
A rabbit reading a newspaper.
Some burnt food.
A blue bird.

Can they see the red lizard?
He's trying to put Mrs Lion's fire out with water.

Pages 44–45

- What are the birds on page 44 travelling in?
  A hot-air balloon.
- Would you like to go in a hot-air balloon?
- What is Mr Crocodile doing?
- Can you drive a car?
- Do you know someone who can drive a car?
- What animals can climb trees?
- Can elephants climb trees?
- Can crocodiles fly?
- What is the bear trying to do?
- How many animals can you see in the water?

Just for fun

Ask the children to find the following things:

An angry-looking spider.
A fish laughing.
A monkey in a tree.
A rabbit running.

Can they see the red lizard?
He's trying to burst the balloon with a pin.

Exercise A

Written. Children fill in the numbers of things they see in the picture. Could also be done orally.

Spiders 2	Birds 4	Mountain 1
Fish 4	Rabbits 4	Coconuts 4
Bees 4	Butterflies 5	Flowers 11

- Extra: ask the children to look at the picture for two minutes. Tell them to close the book and say how many things they can remember.

Exercise B

Oral or written. Children list five things they can do and five things they can't do. Suggested answers:

I can sing. I can dance. I can swim. I can't fly. I can't dive.

- Extra: put the children into pairs. Ask them to find out three things their friend can't do. They then take turns to report back to the class.

Exercise C

Oral or written. Children fill in the gaps.

1 No, I can't. 2 No, I can't. 3 No, I can't.

- Extra: make up a list of false statements about yourself, e.g. *I can fly. I can run a kilometre in five seconds. I can stand on my head for three hours.* Get the children to decide whether you are telling the truth about yourself. They should say: *No, you can't.*

Other things to do

Quick activities

- Bring in a ball. Sit the children in a circle on the floor. Tell them to throw the ball to one another. When a child has the ball, he must say a sentence with **I can** before throwing it to the next person.
- Repeat the above using **I can't**. To vary the game a bit, ask the children to pass the ball round while you play some music on a cassette player. Stop the music at random. The child with the ball must say a sentence.
- Play a game of True or False. Prepare a list of true and false sentences, e.g. *Fish can fly. Dogs can swim. Elephants can jump.* Divide the children into teams and read the sentences to them. The team with the most correct answers wins.
- Play a variation of I Spy. Children take turns to decide on an object and then say, for example: *I can see something beginning with **w*** (a window).

- Ask the children to make different sounds. Ask each child what sound he can make and then ask him to make it, e.g. *I can make a car's noise. I can make a lion's noise*.

Longer activities

- Play a guessing game. Make a list of animals or people with a special ability, e.g. *a footballer, a cook, Superman*. Ask the children to listen carefully while you say two or three sentences about the person or animal, for instance: *I can run fast. I can kick a football*. (A footballer.) The children try to guess who you are.
- Write a long word on the board, e.g. alphabet, crocodile. Ask the children how many other words they can attach to it, for instance you could add egg down to the final **e** in crocodile. Encourage the children to say *I can make a word* before they tell you what it is. Here is an example of this game:

```
          R
          E
    CROCODILE
     A        G
     B        GREEN
     B             O
     I             S
     TIGER         ELEPHANT
```

- Tell the children that they are going to invent a superhero. The superhero can do anything the children want him to do. Write on the board: *Our superhero can . . .* Give the superhero a name. Now ask the children to help you list all the things he or she can do.
- ⊙ Turn this last idea into a class project. Divide the children into pairs or small groups. Give each set of children a large sheet of paper. Firstly, ask them to draw their superhero. Then get them to write a list of things that their hero can do. You could display the finished work on the classroom wall.
- ⊙ Stand the children in a circle. Stand in the circle with them and say, for example, *I can put my arm in the air*. When you say this, raise one arm in the air and leave it there. The child standing next to you also puts his arm in the air. He must now think of something else he can do at the same time and say it, e.g. *I can put both arms in the air*. You must now do the same. The next child raises both arms and thinks of yet another thing he can do and says it, e.g. *I can lift one foot off the ground*. Eventually all the children should be doing the same thing. They need not all be complicated: a child might simply say: *I can smile*. The chances are that you and your class will all fall on the floor, but you should have had fun in the process!
- ⊙ Play an alphabetical version of 'In the Jungle'. Child 1 says: *In the jungle I can see an apple*. Child 2 says: *In the jungle I can see an apple and a bear*. Child 3 says: *In the jungle I can see an apple, a bear and a camel*.
- ⊙ Play a game of Chinese Whispers. Sit the children in a long line. Whisper a sentence such as *I can eat spaghetti with my eyes shut* to the first child. Tell him to whisper it to the next child and so on down the line. The last child shouts out what he has heard. It is almost certain to be wrong, but it's fun.

Parents

- Collect a number of pictures or photographs of people or animals. Try to include some sport stars, singers, cartoon characters. Get your child to make a sentence with **He** or **She can . . .** for each picture, e.g. *He can sing. She can play tennis*.
- Cut twenty-one pieces of paper or card. On ten of them write a mixture of the names of people your child knows and some animals. Write a verb on each of the other ten, e.g. *run, fly, jump, sing, dance, swim*. On the final piece of card write: *can*. Put the **can** card in the middle of a table. Put all the name cards face down on the left and all the verb cards face down on the right. Turn over one name and one verb at a time. Encourage your child to tell you whether the sentence made is true or not, e.g. *Daddy can fly. No, he can't. Mr Lion can run. Yes, he can*.
- Play a variation of I Spy. Don't forget that you can do this almost anywhere: in the car, in the garden, at home. Encourage your child to use **I can** each time, like this: *I can see something beginning with **t*** (tree).
- Challenge your child to think of something he can do but you can't and vice versa, e.g. (Child) *I can stand on my head*. (Parent) *I can drive a car*.
- Extend this idea by taking turns to perform the actions, e.g. (Child) *I can stick my tongue out*. You now imitate him. (Parent) *I can hop ten times*. Your child imitates you.
- Watch television with your child. Encourage him to describe what his favourite television characters can and can't do.
- Invent a new cartoon character with your child. Get some paper and coloured pencils. Ask him to draw the new character. Now help him to decide what his character can do, e.g. *He can run very fast. He can fly an aeroplane. He can drive. He can lift very heavy things*.
- Ask your child to shut his eyes. Tell him (in your own language) to imagine that he is in a very beautiful place. Ask him to describe what he can see and smell and hear. Encourage him to use **I can** at the beginning of each sentence, e.g. *I can see blue sea. I can hear music*. Join in with your child. Take turns to say a sentence each.

Chapter 1 Plural of nouns

Words

box	glass	potato	treasure
coin	map	tomato	watch

Questions to ask children

Pages 4–5

- What is going on in the picture?
  The animals have found some treasure.
- Have you ever found any treasure?
- If so, what was it?
- What is in the boxes?
- Where might the treasure have come from?
- How did the animals find it?
- Did they dig it up?
- Did it come from a shipwreck?
- What has each animal taken from the boxes?
- What do you think is on the secret maps?

Just for fun

Ask the children to find the following things:

Two padlocks.
An animal with a potato peeler.

Can they see the red lizard?
No, this is the picture he's not in.

Pages 6–7

- Where are the animals now?
  They've gone back home with the treasure.
- How many animals are there in the picture?
- If you could have some of the animals' treasure, what would you choose?
- Where would you keep it?
- Who do you think has got the most treasure?
- What do you think the animals are going to do with the fruit and vegetables?
- What do you think they will do with the coins, watches and glasses?

Just for fun

Ask the children to find the following things:

An animal carrying something in his mouth.
An animal wearing glasses (spectacles).

Can they see the red lizard?
He's pulling a bird's tail feathers.

Exercise A

Children study the two crocodiles and say what the differences are. Let children circle the differences in their books. Do this exercise orally first and then in writing to reinforce the plural forms.

1 has got a glass.	2 has got two glasses.
1 has got a watch.	2 has got two watches.
1 has got a necklace.	2 has got two necklaces.
1 has got a map.	2 has got two maps.
1 has got an orange.	2 has got two oranges.
1 has got an apple.	2 has got two apples.
1 has got a potato.	2 has got six potatoes.
1 has got a banana.	2 has got three bananas.
1 has got a coin.	2 has got four coins.

N.B. For those of you who decide to teach irregular plurals at this stage, Crocodile 1 has got nine teeth, Crocodile 2 has only got eight teeth.

◉ Extra: put the children in pairs. Tell them to empty out their schoolbags. They then compare what each of them has got, e.g. *I've got three pencils. You've got two pencils.*

Exercise B

Oral. Children look for the objects in the picture.

◉ Extra: to make this more competitive, divide the class into teams. The first team to find all the objects wins. To check that they really have found them, appoint one child as a spokesman to point them out in the picture.

Exercise C

Oral or written. Children say what each animal has got.

Mr Lion has got a glass and two bananas.
Mr Elephant has got four tomatoes and three boxes.
Mr Rabbit has got two maps and five carrots.
Mr Snake has got two watches and an orange.

- Extra: turn back to pages 4–5. Ask the children to look at each animal and say or write what each one has got.

Exercise D

Written. Children circle all the animals they can find in the word search. The words are written horizontally and vertically only. Remember to point out that they are looking for plurals. The animals in the word search are:

BEARS	BIRDS	ELEPHANTS
HIPPOS	LIONS	MONKEYS
RABBITS	SNAKES	TIGERS

- Extra: make your own word searches using only fruits, or any other vocabulary familiar to your students.

There is one more animal in the word search. He's not in the plural: it's SMUFF (second line down, horizontally).

Other things to do

Quick activities

- Tell the children to turn back to pages 4–5 and to count as many things as they can see. Ask the children questions, e.g. *How many watches are there? How many animals? How many apples?*
- Ask the children to imagine that they have found some treasure. Get them to tell you what their treasure is. Write their suggestions on the board.
- Draw an outline of an island on the board. Tell the children that it is an island on one of the animals' secret maps. Ask them to tell you what to draw on the island, e.g. *houses, rivers, trees, animals, bridges, places where treasure is hidden.*
- Bring in a set of objects, several of each, e.g. books, spoons, photographs, toys. Put them on a table and ask the children to tell you what they are.
- Or turn this into a memory game. Let the children look at the objects for one minute. Cover them and ask the children what they are.
- To make this more difficult, remove a couple of objects at a time and ask the children to tell you what's missing.
- Play a game of Hangman on the board, using only the plural of nouns that are familiar to the children.

Longer activities

- ◉ Put the children into small groups. Tell each group to draw a treasure chest full of the things they would like to find. When they have all finished, ask a member of each group to tell the rest of the class what is in their chest.
- ◉ Or swap all their drawings round so that a different group has to work out what is in the chest.
- ◉ Cut twenty-eight pieces of card. Write a word in the singular on each, e.g. book, apple, tomato, box, lion, mango. Using the remaining eight cards, write four cards which say **S** and four which say **ES**. Divide the children into four groups and give five word cards to each group. Give each group an **S** and an **ES** card. Ask them to make plurals from the words and plural endings that they have, e.g. Box + es. Go round monitoring their progress and making sure they are putting the appropriate ending on each word.
- ◉ Divide the class into groups. Ask each group to draw a set of things, e.g. Group 1 draws five houses, Group 2 draws ten trees. When they have finished, assemble all the drawings, cut them out and stick them onto a large piece of paper on which you've drawn the outline of the island. Label each of the things the children have drawn, e.g. *There are five houses*. Display the finished picture on the classroom wall.
- ◉ Divide the children into pairs or small groups. Tell them that they are going to draw the bedroom of a person called Dr Collector. Dr Collector loves shopping. Every day he goes out to buy something new. However, he has a bit of a problem: he can only buy things in twos. Let the children be as imaginative as they can be, for instance Dr Collector's room might have two sets of pyjamas, two alarm clocks, two cats sitting on the bed, two identical pictures on the wall. Help the children to label the things they've drawn. Ask each pair or group to describe their picture to the rest of the class.

Parents

- Play a game of I Spy with your child. The things you spy must always be plural, e.g. *I spy with my little eye three things beginning with* ***b*** (bananas). You can either do this by using pages in the book, or by looking round your own home. Don't forget that this is a game that can be played anywhere, on a train journey or in the car, for example.
- Do a bit of cooking with your child. As you take each ingredient, ask him to tell you what it is. This would work particularly well if you were making something which required several of the same ingredients, a salad or a fruit salad, for example. Ask: *What are these?* Your child answers, e.g., *They're tomatoes. They're onions.*
- Write a list of words in a column on the left-hand side of a sheet of paper, e.g. book, potato, box, rabbit, car, tomato, toy, friend, mango. On the right-hand side, write a big **S** and a big **ES**. Ask your child to draw lines joining the words with their correct ending to make them plural.
- Tell your child that you are both going to draw an imaginary animal. The animal can be as silly as you like. Take turns to draw bits of the animal. Each time you draw something, say what it is, e.g. *The animal has got five ears. The animal has got three legs. The animal has got two tails*. When the drawing is finished, label all the things you have drawn.
- Play an 'In the Jungle' game. Use only plurals, like this: (You) *In the jungle I see two trees*. (Child) *In the jungle I see two trees and three monkeys*. (You) *In the jungle I see two trees, three monkeys and five bananas*. If you can get other members of the family to join in that would be even better.

BOOK 2 Chapter 2 How many?

Words

arm	foot	skier
ear	leg	snow
eye	monster	snowball
feet	mouth	teeth
finger	ski	tooth

Questions to ask children

Pages 8–9

- Where are the animals?
- What are they doing?
- Have you ever seen snow?
- Where does it snow?
- What can you do with snow? *Build a snowman, have a snowball fight, ski, sledge, build an igloo.*
- How many elephants can you see?
- What are the two animals at the bottom of page 9 doing?
- How many tortoises can you see?
- What is Mr Crocodile doing?

Just for fun

Ask the children to find the following things:

Three animals on a sledge.
Someone crashing into a tree.
A baby tortoise.
A fire.

Can they see the red lizard?
He's throwing snowballs.

Pages 10–11

- What are the animals doing now?
- How many animals are having a hot drink?
- What have the animals built in the snow? *A snow monster.*
- Would you like to go skiing?
- Do you think the animals enjoy the snow?
- How many animals are there in the picture?
- How many animals are on pages 8–9?
- What would you see if Smuff was in the snow? *Just two brown (or black!) ears.*

Just for fun

Ask the children to find the following things:

Two birds wearing hats.
A monkey laughing.
A young elephant.

Can they see the red lizard?
He's having a snowball fight with a rabbit.

Exercise A

Written. Children count up the number of things in the list and fill in the numbers. Clues are given on the mugs that are being held by the animals. Could also be done orally.

10 skis	5 monkeys	3 birds
6 trees	3 rabbits	16 snowballs
2 blue hats	11 red hats	

- Extra: ask the children to look at pages 30–31. Ask how many of the following things they can see: *rabbits, animals with broken legs, crocodiles, nurses.*

Exercise B

Oral or written. Children look around the room and either say or write how many things they can see. Suggested answers:

I can see three friends. I can see ten desks.
I can see eight pictures. I can see five books.

◉ Extra: divide the children into pairs. Tell them to empty out their schoolbags. They then compare how many things each of them has got. Encourage them to take turns to ask and answer questions, like this:
Child 1 *How many pencils have you got?*
Child 2 *I've got three pencils. How many books have you got?*

Exercise C

Written. Could also be done orally. Children look at the snow monster and count the number of fingers, arms etc. he has. Before you do this check that the children know the parts of the body (see 'Other things to do' below).

The snow monster has got:

4 eyes	1 mouth	12 fingers	6 feet
3 arms	6 legs	12 teeth	2 ears

◉ Extra: put the children into pairs. They take turns to test one another on the snow monster, e.g. *How many feet has he got? He's got six feet.*

Other things to do

Quick activities

- Check that the children know the parts of the body. If they don't, draw a stick man on the board and label the parts of the body on it.
- Once they are familiar with the parts of the body, play a game of Mr Tiger Says, a variation of Simon Says, to reinforce the vocabulary, e.g. *Mr Tiger says: Touch your head. Mr Tiger says: Put you hand on your leg* etc. When they are confident with the new words, let them have a go at being Mr Tiger.

- Draw a large circle on the board. Tell the children that it is a monster's body. Ask them to tell you how many arms, legs, eyes, noses, feet etc. to draw.
- Play a game of I Spy, telling them that they can only spy numbers of things, not individual objects. e.g. *I spy with my little eye ten things beginning with* **d** (desks).
- Write up a number of questions on the board, for example: *How many brothers and sisters have you got? How many pets have you got? How many lessons do you have a day? How many toys have you got?*
- Using the rest of the book, make up a little quiz. Ask the children to find the pages on which they would find, e.g. *five red flowers, two elephants, six trees, a blue bird.*
- ◉ To make this kind of game more competitive, divide the children into teams. Whichever team gets the answers correct first wins. You could do this with this chapter in particular, or use other pages in the book.

Longer activities

- ◉ Put the children into small groups. Tell them that you are going to ask them a series of questions. They must write down the answers. Now ask questions like these: *How many rooms are there in your house? How many brothers or sisters have you got? How many pencils are there in your pencil case? How many desks are there in the classroom? How many pupils are there in this class? How many days are there in a week?* Get the children to read out their answers.
- Do a picture dictation. Make sure each child has a piece of paper and a pencil. Slowly say, for example, *In the shop there are three oranges. In the shop there are two bottles. In the shop there is a shopkeeper*. When you have finished ask, e.g., *How many oranges are there in the shop?* The children look back at their drawings and tell you how many of each item there are.
- ◉ Write a list of different kinds of food horizontally across the top of the board, e.g. chocolate, pizza, apples, fish, chicken, salad, rice. Ask each child in turn to say which of the items of food he likes. Keep track of how many children like each thing by drawing a dash on the board each time. When the whole class has answered, ask the children to look at the results and say how many children like each thing, e.g. *Ten children like pizza. Two children like fish.*

Parents

- Make a number poster. Take ten sheets of paper. Ask your child to draw one animal one the first sheet. On the second ask him to draw two animals or people. On the third tell him to draw three things, and so on. When all the drawings are complete, label each one like this: One cat. Five tigers. Ten books. Put the drawings on a wall as a reminder to your child.
- Play a game of True or False. Take turns to look round the room you are in and make sentences about it, e.g. There are three lamps. There are two chairs. There are two newspapers. The other one of you has to say true or false, according to what actually is in the room. You could play this game in the garden or in a park, too.
- Send your child (and a friend, if possible) on a treasure hunt. Give him questions to answer, e.g. *How many bars of soap are there in the house? How many beds are there in the house?* You can also ask him to find certain things, e.g. *Find three things that are blue. Find ten coins. Find two magazines*. If you are able to play this game outside, it would be even better.
- Take turns to play a game, add a number to every sentence you make, e.g. (Parent) *In my house there is a cat.* (Child) *In my house there are two pictures.* (Parent) *In my house there are three bedrooms.*
- Tell your child that you are going to draw a strange animal together. Decide first what the animal should be called. Now take turns to decide what to draw, e.g. three ears, two noses, five legs. Take turns to do the drawing.
- If you know the song *Ten green bottles standing on a wall* sing it with your child to practise counting. If not, try to make up a poem or a song of your own, starting with ten or twenty and working backwards, like this:

  In the jungle there are ten tigers
  Big ones, fierce ones, ten big tigers
  In the jungle there are nine little mice
  Small ones, tiny ones, nine little mice . . .
- Play an 'In the Jungle game'. Start it yourself by saying, for example: *In the jungle I see a tree*. Your child then says *In the jungle I see a tree and two monkeys*. You say *In the jungle I see a tree, two monkeys and three zebras*.
- Devise a mini-quiz based on the book. Make a list of appropriate pages in advance. Ask you child questions, e.g. *How many monkeys are there on page 44? How many tortoises can you see on page 21?*

Chapter 3 Present simple with **he**, **she** and **it**

Words

does	love	o'clock
doesn't	machine	start
eat	make	sweets
like	noise	toy

Questions to ask children

Pages 12–13

- What can you see in the picture?
- Whose machine do you think it is?
- What do you think it makes?
- Do you think this machine makes a lot of noise?
- Would you like a machine like this one?
- Do you think Mrs Lion likes eating sweets?
- What is the rabbit at the bottom of page 13 doing?
  He's putting carrots in the machine to make it work.
- Can you see a clock?
- What time does it say?

Just for fun

Ask the children to find the following things:

Some eggs.
A fish.
A rabbit in a test tube.
Someone wearing a space helmet.
An animal running.

Can they see the red lizard?
He's dropping a rabbit into part of the machine.

Pages 14–15

- Can you see a clock?
- What time does it say?
- Where is Mr Lion?
- Is he awake?
- Does he look tired?
- When does the machine start?
  It starts at eight o'clock.
- At what time do you get up?
- When do you have breakfast?
- Can you see some toys in the picture?
- What toys can you see?

Just for fun

Ask the children to find the following things:

A toy train.
A duck.
A monkey wearing a mask and snorkel.
Someone wearing ear-rings.

Can they see the red lizard?
He's holding onto the balloon.

Exercise A

Written. Could also be done orally. Children fill in the gaps with the verbs provided on the balloon.

1 Mrs Lion cooks breakfast.
2 He plays with the toys.
3 Mr Rabbit puts carrots in the machine.
4 She eats sweets.
5 She reads a book.

- Extra: ask the children a series of 'wrong' questions, e.g. *Does Mr Lion cook breakfast? Does the machine start at nine o'clock?* Encourage them to correct you using the present simple.

Exercise B

Oral or written. Children re-order the rabbit's words to make correct sentences.

1 The machine makes a lot of noise.
2 Mrs Lion likes sweets.
3 It makes sweets and toys.
4 The machine starts at seven o'clock.
5 He loves his machine.

- Extra: write some more jumbled sentences on the board, like these: *carrots likes Mr Rabbit. Breakfast cooks Lion Mrs everyday. toys Mr plays with Crocodile.*

Exercise C

Written. Could also be done orally. Children ask their friends to tell them five things they do everyday. Suggested answers:

He gets up at half past seven. She brushes her teeth. He eats bread and honey. She watches television.

- Extra: ask the children to think about what you do every day. Write their answers on the board, e.g. *Our teacher gets up at a quarter past seven.*

Other things to do

Quick activities

- Tell the children that you know a few things about Smuff which very few people know. Ask the children to tell you whether what you 'know' is true or not. Say the following things, or write them on the board: *Smuff eats bread for his supper* (True). *Smuff has a skateboard* (False). *Smuff likes dandelions* (True). *Smuff has two hutches* (True). *Smuff paints pictures* (False). *Smuff watches television* (True). You can, of course, make up your own sentences about Smuff.

- ⊙ Go round the class asking each child in turn to say one sentence about someone in their family. Tell the children that this must be something the person does everyday, e.g. *My father drinks two cups of coffee. My sister goes swimming. My brother plays football.*
- ⊙ Make this more difficult by telling the children that they cannot repeat an activity that someone else has already mentioned.
- ⊙ Ask the children to think of someone they know. Tell them to say one sentence about that person. The sentence may be true or false. The class tries to decide whether the child is telling the truth or not, e.g. *My friend Francis eats worms. My neighbour goes shopping every day.*
- Ask the children to think about a character in the book, Mr Elephant, for example. Ask each child to say a sentence about what Mr Elephant does every day, like this: *Mr Elephant gets up at seven o'clock. Mr Elephant washes his face. Mr Elephant eats three chocolate cakes for breakfast.*
- ⊙ Ask the children who their favourite actor or cartoon character is. Ask them to tell you why they like him and what he can do. List everything the children say on the board.

Longer activities

- ⊙ Divide the children into pairs. Give each child a piece of paper. Write a selection of verbs on the board, e.g. *washes, gets up, eats, runs, reads, talks* etc. Tell them to write someone's name and a verb on the left-hand side of the paper. Ask them to fold the paper so that the name cannot be seen and to pass it to their partner. Now ask the children to write one of the following phrases on the other side of the paper, *every day, in the morning, at lunch time*. Tell the children to unfold the papers and read their sentences to the class, e.g. *Sarah gets up at lunch time. Mr Crocodile eats in the morning.*
- ⊙ Ask the children to write one sentence about themselves on a slip of paper. Tell them to use the verb **like**. Instead of using their real names they should write a false name. Collect all the papers and read them out one by one. The class tries to guess who has written the sentence. Play the game like this: (You) *'Superman' likes playing football.* (Class) *Is it John?* (You) *No.* (Class) *Is it Peter?* (You) *Yes.*
- Tell the children that you are going to invent a new cartoon character. You are going to describe a typical day in his or her life. Ask the children to give you suggestions. Write them on the board, e.g. *He gets up in the middle of the night. He brushes his two front teeth. He eats three bananas and some ice cream for breakfast.*
- ⊙ Turn this into a bigger project by putting the children into groups and asking them to draw the character, then to list all the things he does.
- ⊙ Bring in a ball. Sit the children in a circle on the floor. Tell them to throw the ball to one another. When you clap your hands, they must stop throwing the ball. Whoever has the ball must say a sentence in the present simple with **he**, **she** or **it**.
- ⊙ To vary this game, bring in a cassette player and use music to determine when the children should stop throwing or passing the ball.
- ⊙ Play a game of Chinese Whispers. Sit the children in a long line and whisper a sentence to the first child, e.g. *Mr Rabbit eats dandelions and carrots*. The sentence is whispered down the line. The last child in the line shouts out what he has heard.
- ⊙ Divide the children into small groups. Give each group a large sheet of paper. Tell the children that they are going to invent the machine of their dreams. Ask them to decide what their machine is going to make. Now tell them to draw a picture of it. When they have finished drawing, ask them to list all the things it does, e.g. *Our machine makes chocolate books. It starts at five o'clock in the morning. It makes a lot of noise. It gets very hot.* Display the machines on the classroom wall.

Parents

- Say a series of 'wrong' statements about this chapter. Say for example, *The machine starts at eleven o'clock. Mrs Lion likes the noise. The machine makes bananas*. Get your child to correct you, using the present simple.
- Make a list of simple sentences about people's everyday habits in your own language. Read them slowly to your child and get him to translate them into English. Make sure that he adds the **s** ending to the verb each time.
- Cut a number of pieces of card. On some of them write the names of animals or friends and family, e.g. *Mr Lion, Daddy, Katya, Mrs Jones*. On others write some verbs, e.g. *reads, eats, sleeps, likes*. Put the cards into two separate piles. Take a card from each pile and ask your child to finish the sentence, e.g. Mr Lion eats . . . might become *Mr Lion eats meat* or *Mr Lion eats at twelve o'clock.*
- Tell your child that you are going to invent a timetable for one of the characters in the book. On a sheet of paper write the following: *At seven o'clock, at eight o'clock, at eleven o'clock, at lunch time, at three o'clock* etc. Now ask your child to think of the things that the character does at those times, e.g. *At seven o'clock Smuff gets up. At eight o'clock he eats breakfast.*
- Play a game of true or false. Say a sentence about someone you and your child both know, e.g. *Mr Smith wears a red hat and blue boots*. Your child decides whether what you have said is true or false. Take turns to say the sentences.

BOOK 2

Chapter 4 **I like** and **I don't like**

Words

bed	ice cream	rice
chicken	meat	salad
cooking	milk	school
eating	pizza	shopping
going	playing	spaghetti
homework	reading	swimming

Questions to ask children

Pages 16–17

- What is happening in the picture?
  The animals are having a feast.
- Is it day-time or night-time?
- How do you know? *There is a moon and coloured lights.*
- Are the animals wearing smart clothes?
- What do you think they might be celebrating?
- Do you sometimes have big meals at home?
- Do you like eating?
- What is your favourite food?
- What are the birds doing? *They're waiters.*

Just for fun

Ask the children to find the following things:

A worried-looking chicken.
A greedy animal with two slices of cake.
Someone eating potatoes.

Can they see the red lizard?
He's hitting Mr Monkey with a cucumber.

Pages 18–19

- How many snakes can you see?
- What sports do you like playing?
- What sports don't you like?
- Do you like school?
- Do you think the animals like going to school?
- What do tortoises eat?
- What do lions eat?
- Do you think the animals like sweets and ice cream?
- What food don't you like?

Just for fun

Ask the children to find the following things:

Two animals with their legs crossed the same way.
Someone holding a sugar cane.
A bar of chocolate.
Three animals sticking their tongues out.

Can they see the red lizard?
He's eating sweets on the branch of the tree.

Exercise A

Oral or written. Children answer the snakes' questions. Either do this as a class, asking each child to answer each question, or ask them to write the answers in their notebooks. Their answers will vary according to their individual preferences.

- Extra: if you have chosen to teach your children **He/She does** or **doesn't like** and **We/They do** or **don't like**, you can extend this exercise by putting the children in pairs or small groups. Ask them to interview each other. They then report their findings back to the class. If not, ask further questions, e.g. *Do you like going on holiday? Do you like painting? Do you like having a bath?*

Exercise B

Written. Children write a list of five things they don't like. Suggested answers:

I don't like tidying my room. I don't like cabbage.
I don't like getting up early. I don't like Maths.

- Extra: the children say five things they like.

Exercise C

Written and oral. Tell the children that the monkeys have made a menu for their new restaurant.
Children tick or cross the things they like or don't like.
Answers will vary according to each child's taste.

- Extra: ask the children to devise a menu of their own. Divide them into small groups or pairs. Tell them to draw and write all the things they want to put on their menus. When they've finished, get them to read their menus to the class.

Exercise D

Written. Children fill in either **I like** or **I don't like** in the gaps provided. Tell the children to look carefully at what the animals are eating and to look especially at their faces.

1 I like sweets.
2 I don't like spaghetti.
3 I like ice cream.
4 I don't like meat.
5 I like salad.
6 I don't like rice.

Other things to do

Quick activities

- ◉ Before the lesson starts, make a list of things that you like and don't like to eat (invent them if you like most things). Write the things at random at the top of the board. Draw two columns and label them **I like** and **I don't like**. Ask the children to look at the list of food and guess which you like and don't like. Each time they guess correctly, write the thing under the appropriate column.
- ◉ Extend this by making another list of things you like and dislike doing.
- ◉ Play a chain game. Start it off yourself by saying, e.g. *I like oranges*. Child 1 says: *I like oranges and pizza*. Child 2 says *I like oranges, pizza and chocolate* and so on.
- ◉ Play a similar game using a ball. Sit the children in a circle and get them to throw the ball to one another. Whoever has the ball must say: *I like* . . . Try to encourage the children not to repeat what someone else has already said.
- ◉ Once they are confident with **I like**, repeat the game using **I don't like**.
- ◉ Play a True or False game. Ask each child in turn to say a sentence with **I like**. He can choose whether it is true or not. The class tries to guess whether what he has said is true or false.
- • Pretend to be one of the jungle animals. Say a sentence about yourself, e.g. *I like carrots*. (Mr Rabbit.) The children guess who you are.

Longer activities

- ◉ Conduct a class survey of the children's likes and dislikes. Write all their answers on the board. See how many similarities there are. Again, you need not be restricted to food only: you can include pastimes as well.
- ◉ Make this into a larger project in two ways. Either ask the children to draw pictures of the food they most like and dislike. When they have finished you can make the drawings into a poster to put on the classroom wall.
- ◉ Or collect together a set of pictures showing different activities, e.g. bicycling, playing football, cooking, reading, watching television. Ask the children to decide which are their favourite and least favourite activities. Make up two posters, one headed **I like**, the other headed **I don't like**, and display them on the wall.
- ◉ Tell the children that the class is going to open a new restaurant. Divide the class into small groups. Give each group a sheet of paper. Ask them to draw and label the tastiest menu they can, using all the things they like most. Display all the menus together on the wall.
- ◉ You can, of course, do the same in reverse by asking the children to invent the most disgusting menu they can. They will probably enjoy this even more. Be prepared for some nasty-sounding dishes!
- ◉ Play a game of Chinese Whispers. Sit the children in a line. Whisper a sentence to the first child, e.g. *I don't like cucumber*. The first child whispers the sentence to his neighbour and so on down the line. The last child shouts out what he's heard. It is often a different sentence, but it is good fun!

Parents

- Make a list of food that you know your child likes and dislikes. Cut up twenty pieces of card and write an item of food on each one. Cut two more pieces of card and write **I like** on one and **I don't like** on the other. Put all the food cards face down on a table. Put the **I like** and **I don't like** cards to the left of them, face up. Turn over the food cards one by one. Encourage him to say a sentence each time, like this: *I like ice cream. I don't like fish.*
- Take turns to think of different things you each like. These can be kinds of food or activities such as swimming or watching television. Start the game by saying, e.g. *I like oranges*. Your child must now say something he likes. Try not to repeat the same things.
- Once your child is confident with **I like**, play the same game using **I don't like**, e.g. *I don't like English. I don't like shopping*. To vary the game a bit, throw a ball to one another as you say each sentence. If you can involve a brother, a sister or a friend to play the game with you, that would be even better.
- Help your child to make **I like** and **I don't like** posters. Get two large sheets of paper. Either ask your child to draw things, or cut pictures out of magazines and newspapers.
- Using pictures from magazines, make up a menu for your child. Encourage him to pretend he is in a restaurant and get him to say, e.g. *I like chicken. I don't like carrots*. Let him pretend to be the waiter, and tell him what you like and don't like.

BOOK 2

Chapter 5 Present simple with **I**, **you**, **we**, **they**

Words

cook	grow	newspaper	swim
every day	lunch	read	talk
garden	morning	shopping	watch

Questions to ask children

Pages 20–21

- What can you see in the picture?
  It's one of the jungle villages where the animals live.
- Who is watching television?
- Who is carrying bags of shopping?
- Can you see some animals cooking?
- What do you think they are cooking?
- What are the tortoises doing?
- Who is still in bed?
- When do you get up?

Just for fun

Ask the children to find the following things:

Someone reading a newspaper.
A chicken ready to be cooked.
A hippopotamus.
An animal wearing a mask and snorkel.

Can they see the red lizard?
He's trying to cut through the television cable.

Pages 22–23

- Where are the animals now?
  They're inside one of the caves on pages 20–21.
- What kind of animals are the ones hanging upside down? *They're bats.*
- When do bats go out? *At night.*
- Have you ever seen a bat?
- What animals are the elephants standing on?
- How many rabbits can you see?
- Do you think the elephants are very heavy?
- Would you like to have an elephant on your shoulders?

Just for fun

Ask the children to find the following things:

A very worried-looking rabbit.
An animal with horns.
Two palm trees.

Can they see the red lizard?
He's trying to catapult a tomato through the gazelle's horns.

Exercise A

Oral or written. Children read and answer the bats' questions. Suggested answers:

Every day I play with my toys.
After school I see my friends.
At eight o'clock I go to bed. (If 8.00 pm.) or
At eight o'clock I have breakfast. (If 8.00 am.)
At lunch time I eat a sandwich.
At three o'clock I play with my friends.

- Extra: ask additional questions, starting at the beginning of the day. Give each child a chance to answer.

Exercise B

Oral or written. Children work out the secret message by looking at the colours of the animals' T-shirts and comparing them with the colour code.

The message reads: MONKEYS EAT BANANAS.

- Extra: make your own secret messages, either using colours or numbers.

Exercise C

Written. Could also be done orally. Children write five true sentences about themselves. Suggested answers:

I get up at seven o' clock. I brush my teeth every day. I go to school. I play with my friends. I like sweets and fruit. I go to the beach once a year. I have a brother.

- Extra: ask each child in turn to say one sentence about himself. The sentence need not be true. The class tries to decide whether it is true or not.

Exercise D

Oral or written. Children decide whether the sentences are true or false.

Birds can swim.	False*
Monkeys like bananas.	True
Rabbits eat carrots.	True
Fish fly in the sky.	False
Elephants are red.	False
Lions run fast.	True

* Actually, some birds can swim but for the purposes of this exercise I suggest you ignore this. Leave it to the science teacher.

- Extra: say several true and false sentences about yourself, e.g. *I speak English. I can run faster than a tiger. I eat caterpillars every day.* Let the children decide whether you are telling them the truth or not.

Other things to do

Quick activities

- ◉ Go round the class asking each child to say one sentence about something he does every day. Start this off yourself by saying, eg., *Every day I wash my hands*.
- ◉ Make this more difficult by asking the children to say a sentence that can be either true or false, e.g. *I eat bread for breakfast. I eat worms for breakfast*. The class guesses whether the child is telling the truth or not.
- ◉ Before the lesson starts, make a list of true and false statements about yourself, e.g. *I climb a mountain every night. I have a cup of tea in the morning. I stand on my head at bedtime. I like milk*. Ask the children to decide whether your statements are true or false. If the children think they are false, they should say, e.g. *No, you don't like milk*.
- ◉ Put the children into pairs. Ask them to talk to each other and find out two things they both do every day. When they have all found out two things, ask them to report their findings to the class, like this: *We like football. We walk to school*.
- Write a list of animals on the board, e.g. *lion, rabbit, elephant, monkey, cat, mouse, dog*. Ask the children to make one sentence about each animal, like this: *Lions run fast. Rabbits have long ears. Monkeys eat nuts*.
- Tell the children that you are going to read some sentences to them. If the statement applies to them, they should stand up. If it doesn't they remain seated. Now read sentences such as the following: *I get up every day* (whole class stands). *I go to bed at eight o'clock* (some sit). *I brush my teeth in the morning. I like apples. I can run fast. I can fly. I eat five onions every day*.

Longer activities

- ◉ This is a variation of Pass the Parcel. Collect lots of used envelopes and scraps of paper. Write a verb on each of the scraps of paper. Put one of the bits of paper inside an envelope. Stick the other verbs to the front of the other envelopes, one on each. Now fold the envelopes and put one inside another until you have a biggish packet. Bring in a cassette recorder and some music. Sit the children in a circle and tell them to pass the parcel round. When the music stops the child with the parcel opens the first envelope. He must make a sentence using the verb that is stuck to the front of the envelope. The parcel is then passed on until all the envelopes have been opened.
- Ask the children to make a fact file about themselves. They should write down all the things they do every day, e.g. *I get up at seven o'clock. I eat breakfast with my brother. I help my parents with the washing-up*.
- ◉ Make this into a bigger project by putting the children into small groups. Give them some paper and ask them to decide on ten things they all do every day. They should write each thing down and draw a picture of the action to go with it. You could display the finished drawings on the wall.
- Play a Yes/No game. A child thinks of something he does every day. The class question him, using questions that can be answered by Yes or No only. Play the game like this: (Child thinks of watching television) *Do you do it in the evening?* Yes. *Do you do it outside? No. Do you like doing it?* Yes.
- ◉ Tell the children that you are going to keep a class diary. Write a list of times on the board, for instance: *at nine o'clock, at break time, at lunch time, at two o'clock, at three o'clock, on Monday, on Thursday* etc. Now get the children to help you fill in what they do at those times, e.g. *On Thursday we have a Maths lesson. At break time we go and play outside*.

Parents

- Tell your child to imagine he is a film star. You are going to interview him about his everyday life. Ask him questions, e.g. *When do you get up? What do you eat for breakfast? What sports do you like? Have you got any brothers or sisters? Do you have a pet?* Encourage him to answer you in English using the present simple, like this: *I get up at eight o'clock*.
- Take a piece of paper and write on it, for example, *lions, apples, rabbits, I, we, dogs, elephants, my parents, my friends*. Ask your child to look at the list and make up one sentence for each of the phrases, e.g. *Lions run fast. My parents are very nice. Dogs chase cats*.
- Play a game with your child, like this: you say, for instance, *I like chicken*. Your child now has to think of something he likes, e.g. *I like pizza*. Try this with **I don't like** and other verbs too, e.g. *eat, read, watch*.
- Ask your child to make a timetable of a typical day in his life. Help him to do this by getting a notebook, or a large sheet of paper and writing on it: *at seven o'clock, at nine o'clock, at eleven o'clock, at lunch time, at three o'clock* etc. Now help him to fill in all the things he does at those times, e.g. *At lunch time I eat sandwiches*. You could ask him to draw pictures to accompany each of the actions.
- Play a game of True or False. Say a sentence, e.g. *I like swimming* or *I can fly like a bird*. Ask your child to tell you whether he thinks you are telling the truth or not.

BOOK 2

Chapter 6 Present continuous

Words

arrow	cowboy	lassoo	wigwam
bow	fall	laugh	zebra
catch	Indian	play	
climb	jump	shoot	

Questions to ask children

Pages 26–27

- What are the animals doing?
  Playing Cowboys and Indians.
- How many cowboys can you see?
- How many Indians can you see?
- Are the animals having fun?
- Can you see a zebra?
- What is happening to Mr Crocodile?
- Who is chasing him?
- Can you see a wigwam?

Just for fun

Ask the children to find the following things:

A rabbit doing a special dance.
A cowboy with an arrow stuck to his head.
A lion cub fanning a fire.
A tortoise wearing a sheriff's badge.

Can they see the red lizard?
He's about to bash a monkey on the head.

Pages 28–29

- Where are the animals?
  They're in a Cowboy and Indian café.
- Who is the barman?
- What is he doing?
- What is the monkey at the bar doing?
- Can you see animals laughing?
- How many different fruit juices are there?
- What is the elephant reading?
- Can you see anyone eating?

Just for fun

Ask the children to find the following things:

Two posters saying 'Reward'.
A dart-board.
A ladder.
A frog.

Can they see the red lizard?
He's on a 'Wanted' poster.

Exercise A

Written. Children fill in the gaps using the present continuous.

1 I'm drinking a milkshake.
2 We're laughing.
3 They're talking.
4 We're playing.
5 I'm reading a book.
6 They're eating sandwiches.

- Extra: mime various actions, e.g. eating, running, sleeping, laughing, talking. Ask the children to tell you what you are doing.

Exercise B

Oral or written. Children find numbers 1–5 and describe what they are doing.

1 She's sleeping.
2 He's eating an apple.
3 He's shooting a bow and arrow.
4 He's falling.
5 He's reading a comic.

- Extra: tell the children to turn back to pages 26–27. Ask questions about the animals not already covered by the text.

Exercise C

Oral or written. Children make as many sentences as they can, using a word from each column. Suggested sentences:

Mr Crocodile's laughing. I'm playing. You're reading.
We're talking. Mr Lion's cooking. She's washing.

⦿ Extra: go round the class asking each child in turn to make up one sentence using **I'm** and the present continuous.

Exercise D

Written. Could also be done orally. Children write the continuous form of the verb.

read, reading
cook, cooking
fall, falling
eat, eating
play, playing
talk, talking

⦿ Extra: make a list of verbs. Divide the class into two teams. Read the verbs out slowly. Tell the children to write the continuous form of each verb. The team who gets the most right wins.

Other things to do

Quick activities

- Play an In the Jungle game. Start it off yourself by saying: *In the jungle I see a tiger reading*. The first child says: *In the jungle I see a tiger reading and a lion sleeping*. The next child says: *In the jungle I see a tiger reading, a lion sleeping and a bear eating*.
- ⊙ Play a chain game. The first child says, e.g. I'm eating. Child 2 says: *You're eating. I'm reading*. Child 3 says: *You're reading. I'm laughing*. Child 4 says: *You're laughing. I'm falling*.
- ⊙ Play a game of Mr Tiger Says. Get all the children to stand up. Clear a space in the room. Say, for instance: *Mr Tiger says I'm running*. The children either run on the spot or run round the room, depending on what you feel you can cope with. Now say: *Mr Tiger says I'm laughing*. The children laugh. Now say: *I'm sitting*. If anyone sits, they are out of the game because you didn't say: *Mr Tiger says . . .*
- Play Hangman. Use only verbs in the present continuous. When you have done two or three on the board, ask the children to think of a verb and come up to the board. The class tries to guess what the verb is.
- Turn to pages 12–13. Ask the children questions about the animals and the machine in the picture, using the present continuous, e.g. *What is Mrs Lion doing? What is the red lizard doing?* Don't forget that you can use almost any page in the book for this purpose.

Longer activities

- ⊙ Cut as many strips of paper as you have children. Write a verb in the present continuous on each piece of paper. Fold all the papers and put them in a box. Ask each child to take one piece of paper and read what is on it. They must not tell anyone else what it says. Now ask each child to come to the front of the class and mime the verb. The class tries to guess what verb is being mimed. They should say, e.g. *You're eating*.
- ⊙ Clear a large space or better still, go outside. Get the children to line up in a long line and hold on to each others' waists. Tell the first child to think of an action in the presents continuous and say it, e.g. *I'm walking*. He should now start walking. The rest of the class copies what he's doing. (They have no choice since they are all joined together.) Once the 'crocodile' of children has been round in a complete circle, it is the turn of the second child to think of an action, e.g. *I'm laughing*. The children all walk round in a complete circle, laughing. Continue until you have run out of verbs and children.
- ⊙ Ask the children each to think of an animal that makes a noise, e.g. a cow, a duck, a lion, a monkey, a dog. Now ask each child in turn to make the noise of the animal he has chosen. The class decides what animal is. They should say either *He's being a duck* or *He's quacking*.
- ⊙ Send one child out of the room. Hide an object – anything you like; it could be a reward of some sort, e.g. a couple of sweets. When it is hidden, ask the child to come back in. Tell him to go round the classroom looking for the hidden object. Tell the rest of the class that they must say the following things, according to how near the child is to the object: You're getting cold. *You're getting warmer. You're getting hot*. Let the child roam round the classroom while the others shout out the appropriate phrase.
- Devise a mini-quiz based on the book. Prepare a list of questions, e.g. *Who is driving a green car on pages 38–39? Who is putting carrots in a machine on page 13?* Get the children to answer you using the present continuous. To make this more competitive, divide the class into two teams. The team with the most correct answers wins.

Parents

- Cut ten pieces of card. On each of the pieces of card write a verb, e.g. *walk, cook, read, fall, play, talk, say, eat, drink, wash*. Now write a separate card that just reads **ing**. Ask your child to see how many sentences he can make by adding the **ing** card to the verb cards, e.g. *I am walking. Mummy is cooking. Daddy is talking*.
- Turn to pages 20–21. Ask your child questions about the animals in the picture, e.g. *What are the monkeys doing? What are the rabbit and the monkey doing? What are Mrs and Mrs Lion doing? Who is cooking lunch? Who is sleeping?*
- Pretend you have no idea what you are doing. Keep asking your child questions, e.g. walk across the room and say: *What am I doing?* Your child should answer: *You're walking*. Now open a book or a newspaper. Ask your child: *What am I doing?* He says: *You're reading*. Get him to watch you doing things in the kitchen and ask him what you're doing. Tell him to use the present continuous, e.g. *You're cooking. You're washing a plate. You're opening the refrigerator*. By the time you've finished, he will be exasperated and think you are mad, but he won't forget how to use this tense.
- Go through some magazines and books and find pictures of people doing various things, e.g. working, cooking, shopping, playing football, eating, standing. Ask you child questions about the pictures and get him to answer, like this: *What is this man doing?* He's drinking a cup of coffee. *What is she doing?* She's playing tennis.

Chapter 7 Possessive adjectives

Words

arm	food	leg
broken	head	lunch
chocolate	hospital	strawberry
flower	hurt	thermometer

Questions to ask children

Pages 30–31

- Where are the animals?
- What is a hospital?
- Have you ever been to a hospital?
- Have you ever hurt yourself?
- Have you ever broken an arm or a leg?
- How many animals can you see with broken legs?
- How many nurses or doctors can you see?
- What do nurses and doctors do?
- How many visitors are there?
- What are the frogs doing?

Just for fun

Ask the children to find the following things:

Someone bringing flowers.
A nurse with a tray of food.
A nurse laughing.
A thermometer.

Can they see the red lizard?
He's examining a plant with a stethoscope.

Pages 32–33

- How many doctors or nurses can you see now?
- Who do you think is the head doctor? *The tiger.*
- Can you see any food in the picture?
- Does it look nicer than the food on pages 30–31?
- Do you like fruit and chocolate?
- What do you think is wrong with the two animals wrapped in bandages?
- Which animal is watching television?
- What do you think he might be watching?
- Do you like watching television?

Just for fun

Ask the children to find the following things:

An animal with a bad eye.
A watch. *On the nurse's shirt.*
Two brothers sharing a bed.
A ball.

Can they see the red lizard?
He's trying to undo the fox's bandage.

Exercise A

Written. Can also be done orally. Children fill in **His** or **Her**.

1 His arm hurts.	4 Her ear hurts.
2 His leg hurts.	5 His tail hurts.
3 His head hurts.	6 Her eye hurts.

◉ Extra: get the children to mime various illnesses. The rest of the class tries to guess what is wrong. You can practise **your** with this exercise, as well as **his** and **her**, by getting the class to say, e.g., *Your stomach hurts.*

Exercise B

Oral or written. Children say or write what their favourite television programme is.

- Extra: ask the children what their favourite foods, sports, colours etc. are.

Exercise C

Oral. Children guess the animal being described.

Mr Crocodile. Mr Elephant.

- Extra: turn to other pages in the book, e.g. 12–13. Tell the children to open their books at the same page. Slowly start to describe one of the characters using the first person. Children try to guess which animal you are describing.

Exercise D

Oral or written. Children look at the objects on the bears' bedside table and say or write the answers. You could also practise **their** by asking the children to say or write: *Their favourite things are . . .*

Your favourite things are:

chocolate	bananas	apples	strawberries
pineapple	grapes	balls	books

- Extra: choose two or three other characters from the book, e.g. *Mrs Monkey, Mr Lion, Mrs Crocodile.* Ask the children to say what they think the animals' favourite things would be.

Other things to do

Quick activities

◉ Bring in a ball and sit the children in a circle on the floor. Tell the children to throw or pass the ball to one another. Whoever has the ball has to say: *My favourite animal is . . .* The next child must think up a different animal. You could do this with a number of different things, e.g. colours, names, food.

- ⊙ Divide the board into three columns. In the far left-hand column write: *my, your, his, her, our, their*. In the middle column write: *head, hand, ear, tummy, leg, finger, nose, foot*. In the third column write: *hurts*. Now go round the class asking each child to make up a sentence using a word from each of the columns, e.g. *My tummy hurts*. Make sure they make the nouns plural where appropriate.
- ⊙ Cut as many strips of paper as you have children. On each strip of paper write a sentence, e.g. *My leg hurts*. Ask each child in turn to get up and mime what is on their piece of paper. The class tries to guess what is wrong with the child in question.
- Ask the children to say one thing they like about the person sitting next to them, using **your**. A child might say, for example: *I like your shirt* or *I like your eyes*. Start this off yourself by saying various things about members of the class.
- Ask the children to think of someone they all know. Tell them that they are going to describe that person. Decide as a class who it is going to be, e.g. *The Headmaster*. Write the children's suggestions up on the board, e.g. *His hair is brown. His eyes are blue. We like his smile. His clothes are smart*.
- Play a Yes/No game. Ask each child to think of either a person or an animal from the book. The class asks questions that can be answered by Yes or No only. Play the game like this: (Child thinks of Mr Crocodile.) The class asks questions such as these: *Are you an animal? Are you a big animal? Do you have teeth? Is your skin green? Is your name Mr Crocodile?*

Longer activities

- ⊙ Do a class survey of all the things that the children consider to be their favourites. This could include: animals, food, sport, people, games, lessons, colours, clothes, places, films or television programmes. Turn this into a project by splitting the children into small groups and asking them to draw pictures of the things. You could then make up a poster to put on the wall.
- ⊙ Ask two children to leave the room. Tell them that once they are out of the room they should swap an item of clothing with one another; they might swap jumpers, for example. When they are ready they should come back into the classroom. The class tries to identify what they have swapped. Encourage them to say: *Their jumpers are different* or *Their shoes are different*. You could also ask the children to use objects as well or instead of clothes.
- ⊙ Give one child a piece of paper with the name of an animal written on it (or whisper to the child). Tell him to keep it secret from the rest of the class. The class asks questions to try to discover who the child is: e.g. *Is your neck long? Have you got big ears?* The child who guesses correctly becomes the next animal.

Parents

- To make sure that your child understands the concept of possessive adjectives, say some sentences in your own language, e.g. *My name is Sonya. My eyes are blue. My address is 12 Broad Street*. Ask your child to translate the sentences into English for you.
- Ask your child to say some things about his appearance using **my . . .** It may help if you both stand in front of a mirror. This will prompt your child to think of things to say, e.g. *My hair is brown. My nose is short. My eyes are blue. My shoes are black. My ears are small*. Take turns to say a sentence each.
- Now ask your child to describe you or another member of your family using **your . . .** or **his . . .** or **her . . .**, like this: *His smile is nice. His face is kind. Her hair is long*.
- Watch television together. Encourage your child to describe the characters in the programme using possessive adjectives.
- Make up a mini-quiz based on information your child has access to such as facts about the house, the family or the town you live in. Give him a list of questions to answer, e.g. *What's your brother's name? Where is our television? Who is your teacher? Where are your toys? Where does our dog live?* Encourage him to answer the questions using **my** and **our**, like this: *My toys are in my bedroom. Our dog lives in the garden*.
- Turn to a page in the book, e.g. 40. Ask questions about the animals on the page, for instance: *Are Mr Crocodile's teeth sharp? Is his car green?* Encourage your child to answer by saying, e.g. *Yes, his teeth are sharp. No, his car is red*.
- Extend this by asking similar questions about people you both know, e.g. *Is Granny's house very big?* No, her house is small. *Is Mummy's hair long?* No, her hair is short.
- Mime a series of illnesses, e.g. hold your head and make a face to indicate that you are in pain, walk with a limp, put a scarf round one arm as if it were in a sling. Say to your child: *What is wrong?* Your child answers: *Your head hurts*. Once he is confident, get him to mime some illnesses for you to guess.

Chapter 8 Questions and short answers with **be**

Words

beach	house	sea
castle	hungry	shark
fishing	pirate	shell
friend	sand	water
hot		

Questions to ask children

Pages 34–35

- Where are the animals?
- What do people do at the beach?
  Build sand castles, sunbathe, swim, fish, play games.
- Have you ever been to the seaside?
- What did you do there?
- What did you enjoy most?
- What is a pirate?
- What do pirates usually travel in? A boat.
- Can you see a pirate in this picture?
- What else can you see?

Just for fun

Ask the children to find the following things:

A rabbit in a rubber ring.
Two lion cubs playing ball.
A penguin trying to catch a fish.
A starfish.

Can they see the red lizard?
He's going to tip a bucket of cold water onto the monkeys.

Pages 36–37

- Where are the animals now?
  They're all either in or under the water.
- What colour is the water?
- What can you see underwater?
- Can you see Smuff?
- Do you think he's a good swimmer?
- Can you see a shark?
- Is he a friendly shark?
- Have you ever seen a shark or a dolphin?

Just for fun

Ask the children to find the following things:

A seahorse. A monkey wearing a mask and snorkel.
A lobster.

Can they see the red lizard?
He's trying to sink Smuff's rubber ring by sticking a harpoon into it.

Exercise A

Oral. Can also be done as a written exercise. Children ask each other three questions and take turns to answer, using short answers with **be**. Suggested questions and answers:

1 *Is your name Richard?*	*No, it isn't.*
2 *Are you a boy?*	*Yes, I am.*
3 *Is your hair brown?*	*Yes, it is.*
4 *Am I your friend?*	*Yes, you are.*
5 *Is she the teacher?*	*No, she isn't.*

- Extra: ask the children to ask you questions, e.g. *Are you a teacher? Is your name Bridgid?*

Exercise B

Oral or written. Children match the answers to the questions by following the fishes' bubbles. The bubbles have been made different sizes and colours to make this a bit easier. Children could draw along the bubbles in their books.

1 Are you my friend?	Yes, I am.
2 Is the water blue?	Yes, it is.
3 Are they shells?	Yes, they are.
4 Is she a fish?	Yes, she is.
5 Is he a shark?	Yes, he is.

- Extra: turn back to pages 34–35. Point at various animals and ask questions which elicit answers such as: *Yes, he is* or *Yes, they are* etc. Point at the crocodile and ask: *Is he a crocodile?*

Exercise C

Oral or written. Children answer the questions.

1 Is she a lion?	No, she isn't.
2 Is he a monkey?	No, he isn't.
3 Am I a rabbit?	No, you aren't.
4 Are they crocodiles?	No, they aren't.
5 Is it a football?	No, it isn't.

◉ Extra: bring a group of children up to the front of the class. Ask the 'wrong' questions, e.g. *Is her name Kenna? Is Antony a girl? Is he fifteen years old?* etc. Get the rest of the class to answer the questions you ask.

Other things to do

Quick activities

◉ Go round the class asking 'silly' questions, point at one of the children and say, e.g. *Is he a girl? Is she a doctor? Is he fifteen years old?* Encourage the children to correct you by saying: *No, he* or *she isn't.*

- ◉ Play a chain game with the children. Start it off yourself by asking a child a question such as: *Are you Mark?* The child answers: *Yes, I am*. He must now turn to the child next to him and ask a question, e.g. *Are you six years old?* The child answers and asks his neighbour a question. Continue until everyone has had a chance to answer and ask a question.
- ◉ To vary this, bring in a ball and ask the children to throw it to one another. When you clap your hands or blow a whistle, the child with the ball thinks of a question and asks it. He then throws the ball to the person he wants to answer the question.
- ◉ Play a guessing game. Think of a character in the book, e.g. Mr Lion. Pretend you are that character and say a sentence about him or her, e.g. *I am fierce*. The children try to guess who you are by asking, e.g. *Are you Mr Rabbit?* You answer: *No, I'm not*. When the children are confident enough, get them to think of an animal. You could use people that are known to the whole class, too.
- Mime having a headache in front of the class. Clutch your head in your hands and make a face as if you were in great pain. The children try to guess what's wrong with you by asking, e.g. *Are you ill? Have you got a headache?* Get the children to mime things, too. They don't have to be illnesses, they could be neutral or pleasant things, e.g. being hungry, being happy.
- Cut lots of pictures of people, animals and objects out of old magazines or newspapers. Stick them all on to a large sheet of paper to make up a collage. Stick this on the wall. Point at various things on the poster and ask questions, e.g. *Is it a cat? Is it a car? Is it a man?* Get the children to answer you using short answers.

Longer activities

- ◉ Divide the class into groups. Make sure the groups are sufficiently far apart not to be able to see what other groups are doing. Give each group a list of things to draw, e.g. a house, a forest, a beach ball, a caterpillar. Make sure each group has a different list. Now ask the child to draw the things on one large sheet of paper. When all the groups have finished, swap the drawings round. Each group looks at the drawings they have been given and tries to decide what they are. Encourage them to ask questions. The group whose drawing it is answers by saying, *Yes, it is* or *No, it isn't*.
- ◉ Use the same idea by asking each child in turn to think of an object. The child draws the object on the board. The rest of the class tries to guess what it is.
- Bring in several common objects, e.g. a newspaper, a lemon, a can of lemonade, a box of matches, a passport. Put them in a bag one at a time without the children seeing you. Ask each child in turn to put his hand in the bag and feel the object. He should try to guess what it is.
- ◉ Extend this by getting the child to describe the object he is feeling to the rest of the class, e.g. *It is round. It is hard.* (An apple.) The class tries to guess what the object in the bag is.
- Go round the classroom pointing at various things. Ask a question each time. For example, point at a book and say *Is this Smuff?* Point at a chair and say *Is this a desk?* Get the children to correct you by using short answers.

Parents

- Sit with your child and look at a photograph album. Ask questions about the people and places in the photographs, like this: *Is this Daddy? Is this a beach? Is this a mountain?* Encourage your child to reply using either *Yes, it is* or *No, it isn't*.
- Watch television together. Take turns to ask and answer questions about the programme you are watching, e.g. *Is that Mickey Mouse?* Yes, it is. *Is he old?* No, he isn't. *Has he got black ears?* Yes, he has.
- Cut pictures of ordinary objects out of magazines. Stick them together on a large piece of paper. Cover up part of the object and see if your child can guess what the object is, e.g. *Is it a train? Is it an aeroplane?* Encourage him to ask as many questions as possible. Try to remember to use short answers when replying to his questions.
- Turn to other pages in the book, 12–13 for example. Ask your child questions about the things in the picture. Point at each thing in turn and ask, e.g. *Are they toys? Is that a fish? Are those carrots?*
- Next time you are cooking a meal, get your child to sit with you. Pretend that you have lost your memory and cannot remember the name of anything in the kitchen. Point at the cooker and say: *Is that the washing machine?* Point at a tomato and say: *Is that a banana?* Get your child to correct you every time you get it 'wrong'. It will amuse him and help him to remember the structures. Even you might find it amusing. Once your child seems confident, get him to pretend to have forgotten everything. Answer his questions using short answers. You could play this almost anywhere: in the house, the garden, on the way to school.

Chapter 9 Possessives

Words

beak plane result slow
fast race skateboard wheel

Questions to ask children

Pages 38–39

- What do you think the animals are doing?
  They're having their annual jungle race.
- What kinds of vehicle can you see?
- Do you often see cars like these?
- Who do you think is going to win the race?
- Who would you like to win the race?
- Which do you think is the best vehicle?
- What do you think the monkeys on page 39 are supposed to be doing? *They're mechanics.*
- If you could have any vehicle, what would it be?

Just for fun

Ask the children to find the following things:

A bowlful of fish.
A car with a sail.
Two baby tigers.
An umbrella.

Can they see the red lizard?
He's cheating by trying to slip under the winning tape.

Pages 40–41

- Who do you think won the race?
- What do you think the tortoise's job is?
- Who is looking at Mr Crocodile's car?
- Do you think Mr Crocodile's car is very fast?
- What colour is Mr Snake's car?
- Do you think Smuff owns a car?
- What colour do you think it is?
- Do you think Smuff is a good driver?
  No, he's a terrible driver.

Just for fun

Ask the children to find the following things:

A can of oil.
Two birds.
A number.

Can they see the red lizard?
He's putting carrots into the exhaust pipe of Mr Crocodile's car.

Exercise A

Oral. Children describe Mr Crocodile's car.
Suggested answers:

Mr Crocodile's car is red.
Mr Crocodile's car is new.
Mr Crocodile's car is fast.
Mr Crocodile's car is number 1.
Mr Crocodile's car has got an umbrella on it.

- Extra: ask the children to look back at pages 38–39 and describe another of the animals' cars. To reinforce this exercise, ask the children to write the descriptions in their notebooks.

Exercise B

Oral or written. Children look at the cards and decide what each one is.

1 It's Mr Monkey's tail.
2 It's Mr Snake's tongue.
3 It's a bird's beak.
4 It's Mr Lion's mane/fur.
5 It's Mr Crocodile's mouth.
6 They're a rabbit's ears.

◉ Extra: ask each child to give you something that belongs to them, e.g. a watch, a pencil, a jacket. Show each item in turn to the class and ask: *Whose is this?* The children answer by saying, e.g. *It's Stewart's watch.*

Exercise C

Written. Children look at the pictures and write underneath whose car it is.

1 It's the lions' car.
2 It's Mr Snake's car.
3 It's the monkeys' car.
4 It's Mr Rabbit's car.

- Extra: turn back to pages 38–39. Point at each of the vehicles and ask the children to tell you who they belong to, e.g. *It's Mr Rhinoceros's car.*

Exercise D

Oral or written. Children look at the things around them and say whose they are. Suggested answers:

It's the teacher's desk.
That's Richard's jacket.
These are my friend's pencils.

◉ Extra: ask each child in turn to draw a part of an animal on the board. The class tries to guess what it is, e.g.
Is it a lion's tail?

Other t ings to do

Quick a tivities

- ⊙ Go ro d the class asking each child to tell you the nam a member of their family, e.g. *My brother's name is P y. My cousin's name is James.*
- W this list on the board: *teacher, friend, grandfather, d r, neighbour, school.* Ask the children to copy the list i their notebooks. Now ask them to write in the propriate names, like this: *My teacher's name is r Morgan. My friend's name is Richard.*
- ⊙ xtend this by putting the children into pairs. Ask them to swap notebooks. They then tell the class what their partner has written, e.g. *His doctor's name is Dr Leaver.*
- Draw parts of animals of the board, e.g. a rabbit's tail, a duck's beak, a bird's tail feathers. If you don't like drawing, cut pictures out of old magazines, or trace pictures from books. Ask the children to guess what they are by saying, e.g. *It's a giraffe's neck.*
- Extend this by finding pictures of various objects that the children will be familiar with, e.g. a car, an aeroplane, a boat. Cut out a section from each picture, for instance just the wheel of a car, the sail of a boat, the wing of an aeroplane. Ask the children to identify the sections. Encourage them to say, e.g. *It's an aeroplane's wing.*
- ⊙ Ask the children to look at pages 38–39 again. Tell the children to choose one of the vehicles. They must not tell anyone else which one they have chosen. Ask each child to say two things about the vehicle he has chosen, e.g. *It has an anchor. It has four animals in it.* The class tries to guess which vehicle is being described by asking, e.g. *Is it the seals' car?* (Yes, it is.)

Longer activities

- Ask children to bring in a photograph of themselves. Tell them that they must get their parents' permission to have it. This is because by the time you have finished with it, it won't really be usable again. Mount all the photographs at random on a large sheet of card. Using some white sticky labels, blank out all the children's eyes. Now ask the children to look carefully at each photograph and try to identify whose face it is. They should say, e.g. *It's Frederick's face.* If you want to make this exercise more difficult, cover up other parts of the children (the whole head, for example).
- Extend or vary this by asking for photographs of other personal possessions, e.g. houses, pets, toys. See if the children can guess whose is whose.
- Tell the children that you are going to work out Smuff's family tree. Do this as a class on the board. Write Smuff in the middle of the board. Now get the children to help you to add in other members of Smuff's family. You can extend this as much as you like, include parents, grandparents, brothers, sisters, wife, children, aunts and uncles. Get the children to give each of the family members a name. You can then practise saying, e.g. *Smuff's father's name is Wilfrid. His mother's name is Margaret.*
- ⊙ You could turn this into a bigger project in two ways. Either divide the children into groups and ask each group to draw a number of members of Smuff's family. When the family tree is complete, label each rabbit and stick the finished poster on the wall.
- Or ask the children to do their own family trees. They should write on each one, for instance, *My brother's name is Patrick. My mother's name is Eileen.*
- Tell the children that you are going to imagine the house of a famous inventor. Ask the children to give the inventor a name. Now ask for suggestions as to what his house is like, what he keeps in it and what sorts of thing he invents. Write their suggestions on the board, e.g. *Dr Latherum's house is big and dark. He has a pet kangaroo. The kangaroo's name is Thumper.*

Parents

- Ask your child to think of all the members of your family, including grandparents, aunts, uncles and cousins. Now ask him to tell you the name of each one, using the possessive form, like this: *My uncle's name is . . .*
- Ask your child to think of a house you both know. Tell him to say several things about it, e.g. *My friend's house has got a blue door. My friend's house has got a small garden.* See if you can guess which house he is describing. Take turns to do the describing.
- Cut pictures of people, objects and animals out of old magazines. Either cut a section out of each one, or cover up most of the picture with a piece of paper. See if your child can guess what the object is. Encourage him to say, for example, *It's a man's face. It's an elephant's trunk.*
- Turn to pages 38–39. Ask your child to describe several of the vehicles. Say to him, for instance, *Can you describe the lion's car?* He should try to describe it by saying, e.g. *The lion's car has got a sail. The lion's car has got a number 5 on it.*
- Ask your child to imagine what Smuff's house might be like. Encourage him to draw it. When he has finished drawing, ask him to tell you about it, like this: *Smuff's house has a big garden full of carrots. Smuff's bedroom is painted blue and yellow.*

BOOK 2 **Chapter 10** Possessive pronouns and **these** or **those**?

Words

hat	shoe	these
hers	skirt	those
his	sock	trousers
mine	T-shirt	yours
ours	theirs	

Questions to ask children

Pages 42–43

- What do you think the animals are doing?
  They are having a fashion show.
- How many animals can you see on the stage?
- Can you see someone wearing a hat?
- What is funny about the hat?
  It has got holes for the rabbit's ears to go through.
- Do you think Smuff has a hat?
- Which animal is wearing long socks?
- Who is wearing a skirt?
- Do you think the jungle animals like dressing up?
- Would you like to be in a fashion show?

Just for fun

Ask the children to find the following things:

Two animals arguing.
Three pairs of shoes.
Mr Elephant's shoes.

Can they see the red lizard?
He's pulling Mr Elephant's trouser leg.

Pages 44–45

- What can you see in the picture?
- How many monkeys are there?
- What are they doing?
  They're standing on each other's shoulders.
- Can you see a tiger?
- What is he holding in his paw?
- Can you see a scarf?
- Which animal has got two pairs of trousers?
- Where are Mr Elephant's shoes?

Just for fun

Ask the children to find the following things:

Two rabbits wearing hats.
A butterfly.
A funny pair of shoes.

Can they see the red lizard?
He's hiding behind a tree trunk.

Exercise A

Written. Children match the sentences by drawing lines. Could also be done orally.

It's my sock.	It's mine.
It's his shoe.	It's his.
They're our skirts.	They're ours.
Those are their hats.	They're theirs.
It's her dress.	It's hers.
It's your T-shirt.	It's yours.

◉ Extra: take five objects from five different children. Say, for example: *This is Patrick's pencil*. Encourage the children to say *It's his*.

Exercise B

Oral or written. Children work out what the secret message is by looking at the scarf and the colour code.

The secret message is: THESE SHOES ARE MINE.

- Extra: make your own messages, either using colours or numbers. If the children are confident enough with the language, ask them to invent their own secret messages.

Exercise C

Written or oral. Children make as many sentences as they can, using a word from each of the columns. Suggested answers:

This skirt is yours. These trousers are his.
That dress is hers. Those socks are theirs.

◉ Extra: write the possessive pronouns at random on the board. Go round the class asking each child to invent one sentence using one of the pronouns, e.g. *This book is mine*.

Exercise D

Written. Could also be done orally. Children fill in the gaps using a possessive pronoun.

This is my T-shirt.	It's mine.
This is Mrs Lion's dress.	It's hers.
These are Mr Monkey's trousers.	They're his.
These are Mr Elephant's shoes.	They're his.
This is my skirt.	It's mine.
These are our hats.	They're ours.

◉ Extra: play a game. Child 1 points at an item of his clothing and says, for example: *This is my shirt*. Child 2 must think of a different item of clothing and say, e.g. *These are my trousers*. Child 3 says *These are my shoes* etc.

Other things to do

Quick activities

- Draw two columns on the board. On the left-hand side write this list, vertically: *my, our, their, his, your, her*. On the right-hand side write this list, also vertically: *theirs, hers, mine, ours, yours, his*. Now ask for volunteers to come up to the board and draw a line connecting the two corresponding words, e.g. *my, mine*.
- Go round the class and take something off each child's desk. Ask: *Is this mine?* The children should answer by saying: *No, it's mine*.
- Put the children into pairs. Ask them to empty out their schoolbags. Now tell them to mix up the contents of their bags. When they have done this ask them to pick up each object in turn and decide whose it is. They should ask and answer questions, like these: *Is this pencil yours?* Yes it is. *Is this book mine?* No, it's mine.
- Ask all the children to give you something that belongs to them. Collect them together and put them on a table at the front of the class. Hold up each object in turn and say: *Whose is this?* The children should answer by saying *It's mine* or *It's his* or *hers*.
- Ask each child to point at some things that belong to them. Encourage them to say, e.g. *These are mine. These shoes are mine. These books are mine*. Make sure that they have understood fully that **these** and **those** are used with plurals.

Longer activities

- Bring in a ball. Stand at the front of the class. Throw the ball to one of the children and say a sentence, e.g. *This is my house*. The child who catches the ball must say: *It's mine*. He now throws the ball back to you. Throw the ball to another child and say, e.g. *This is Peter's book*. The child says: *It's his*. Continue this until the children are entirely confident of the use of the possessive pronouns.
- Once you have decided that the children know how to use the pronouns, play the game with the ball again. This time, sit the children in a circle and ask them to make up their own sentences. You may like to give them a theme, e.g. toys, the classroom, the home, in order to help them think up their own sentences. They should say, for example, *This is my teddy*. It's mine. *This is your train set*. It's yours.
- Divide the children into pairs. Ask them to draw a picture of their bedroom. When they have finished drawing, tell them to swap pictures with their partner. They then describe the bedrooms to one another, using **your** and **yours**, e.g. *This is your bed. Those books are yours*.
- Divide the children into small groups. Tell them that they are going to draw the castle of an ancient king. Tell them to be as imaginative as they can be. They can draw the king's soldiers, animals, buildings etc. When they have finished, ask one child in each group to act as a spokesman and describe the castle to the class, like this: *These are his soldiers. This is his horse. This is his throne*. Now take the picture and point at things in it. Say 'wrong' sentences about each thing, e.g. point at the throne and say: *This is the queen's throne. It's hers*. The children correct you by saying: *No, it's his*.
- Ask the children to stand in pairs facing each other. Ask them to point at parts of their partner's body and clothing and say what each thing is, e.g. *This is your face. This is your nose. They're yours. These are your ears. They're yours. This is your shirt. It's yours*.

Parents

- Cut twelve pieces of card. On six of them write *my, your, his, her, our, their*. On the other six write *mine, yours, his, hers, ours, theirs*. Mix them all up and ask your child to make them into pairs, e.g. *my, mine*.
- Collect together ten items which belong to your child and ten which belong to you. Pick each one up in turn and say: *Whose is this? Mine or yours?* Your child should say either *It's mine* or *It's yours*.
- Turn to pages 12–13. Make a list of questions to ask about the picture. Point at Mr Lion's glasses (for example) and say: *Are these my glasses?* Your child answers by saying: *No, they're his glasses*. Point at Mrs Lion's dress and say: *Is this her dress?* Your child answers by saying: *Yes, it's hers*. Point at the machine and say: *Is this her machine?* Your child says: *No, it's his*.
- Go into your child's bedroom. Ask him to tell you about all the things that belong to him. Encourage him to use possessive pronouns, like this: *This bed is mine. These toys are mine. Those books are mine*.

How to play the games

The rabbit game BOOK 1, PAGES 24–25

To play this game you need dice and some counters. The counters can be anything: small buttons for instance, but they must be different colours. You could make your own counters with small squares of coloured card.

The game starts with the counters on the start rock. Players take turns to shake the dice and move onto the appropriate rock. When they land on a rock which has an instruction on it, they must carry out the instruction, e.g. if a player lands on a rock that says: *Lie down!* he must lie down before he can continue to play. If the player gets the instruction wrong, he misses a turn. The winner is the player who reaches the FINISH rock first.

This game can go on for as long as you can bear it. It can be played over and over again since you will inevitably land on different rocks each time.

Where is the red lizard?
He's pointing in two directions at the same time to try to confuse the lost rabbits.

Teachers

You can play this game in three ways:

1 Divide your class into pairs and tell them to play the game with one another. If you choose to do it this way, you will need to walk round the classroom monitoring the children. Make sure that they understand how to play the game and that they understand each of the instructions on the rocks.

2 Divide the class into small groups, perhaps four children in each group. Again, you will need to check that they are playing the game correctly.

3 Play the game as a class. You won't need a counter for this. Let each child have a turn at shaking the dice. The child shouts out the number on the dice. The children count the rocks and put their fingers on the correct rock. Read the instruction aloud to the class. The children now carry out the instruction, e.g. if the rock says: *Draw a rabbit* the whole class has to draw a rabbit. If the rock says: *Laugh!*, make the whole class laugh as riotously as possible.

Parents

If you can persuade other members of the family to join in, you will enjoy this game even more. However, you can easily play the game with your child and no one else.

Put your counters on the START rock. Take turns to shake the dice. Move your counter according to the number shown on the dice. When you land on a rock with an instruction on it, you must do whatever it says before continuing to play, e.g. if your child lands on a rock which says: *Stand up and sit down 3 times* he must do that before he can play again. If he gets the instruction wrong, he misses a turn. Whoever reaches the FINISH rock first wins the game.

The lizard game BOOK 1, PAGES 46–47

To play this game you need dice and some counters. (See 'The rabbit game' above.)

Start with the counters on the START square. Players take turns to shake the dice and move their counter to the appropriate square. Each time they land on a square, they add that word to the list on page 47. They go on until they reach the FINISH square. The list contains essential words needed to form sentences. The players look at the list that they have made. They then make up as many sentences as they can. When everyone has finished, the players read out their sentences.

Here are some possible sentences:

Mrs Giraffe is tall. She has got three yellow bananas.
This rabbit is bad. There is a book under the table.
Who has got an orange? Where is the little rabbit?

Where is the red lizard?
He's cutting Mr Lion's mane.

What is Smuff doing?
He's holding a sign which reads SPA. This stands for the Society for the Protection of Animals.

Teachers

You can play this game in four ways:

1 Divide your class into pairs and tell them to play the game with one another. If you choose to do it this way, you will need to walk round the classroom monitoring the children. Make sure that they understand how to play the game. You may like to suggest that they write their words on a piece of scrap paper if they run out of room on the list provided.

2 Divide the class into small groups, perhaps four children in each group. Again, you will need to check that they are playing the game correctly.

3 Divide the class into two teams. Give each team a counter and dice. The teams play the game until they reach the FINISH box. They then make as many sentences as they can. Set a time limit. When the time has expired ask the children to take turns to read their sentences aloud. Keep a score on the board. Every correct sentence scores one point. The team with the most points wins the game.

4 Play the game as a class. Write the words that are already on the list on the board. Let the children take turns to shake the dice. Ask them to call out the word that you have landed on. Add this to the list on the board. When you reach the FINISH square, ask the children to look at all the words on the board. Go round the class asking each child to make up one sentence.

Parents

Either get other members of the family to join in, encourage a friend of your child's to play, or play this game with just your child.

Put your counters on the START square and take turns to shake the dice. Move your counter to a square according to the number on the dice. Add the word that you land on to the list on page 47. When you reach the FINISH square, look at your lists. See how many sentences you can each make from the words you've got. Take turns to read them to one another. Whoever has the most sentences wins the game.

Jungle fun BOOK 2, PAGES 24–25

To play this game you need counters, dice and an ability to cope with chaos.

The games starts with the counters at the beginning of the path (marked START). Players take turns to shake the dice and move their counters accordingly. They must carry out every instruction they land on, e.g. If the text says: *Stamp your feet* the player must stamp his feet. If it says: *Roar like a lion*, he must roar like a lion.

Some of the pictures along the path are designed to give the players clues as to what to do, for example, next to the instruction *Move your ears*, you will see two rabbits trying very hard to move their ears.

This game can be played indefinitely, or for as long as your nerves can stand it. Encourage the players to participate whole-heartedly.

Where is the red lizard?
He's poking a sleeping monkey with a fork.

Teachers

I think this game is best played as a class. Let the children take turns to throw the dice and read the instructions. Make sure they understand the text and that they do the actions before the dice is shaken again.

You can, of course, play the game in pairs, in small groups, or by dividing the class into two teams. If you decide to do it in one of these ways, you will need to go round the class helping the children and making sure that they are playing the game properly. Give each pair or group dice and counters. Explain to them that they must take turns to play. Tell them that each action has to be performed before the next player has his turn.

Parents

This game will be great fun if you can bribe other members of the family or friends into playing it with you. It will be just as effective if only you and your child can play.

Put your counters at the beginning of the path (marked START). Take turns to shake the dice. Move your counter along according to the numbers on the dice. Each time you land on the text you must perform the action. Encourage your child to read the text carefully and make sure that he understands it. Look at the drawings alongside parts of the text for more clues. The player who reaches FINISH first is the winner.

Smuff's puzzles BOOK 2, PAGES 46–47

Teachers and Parents

These pages comprise six puzzles. They are as follows:

1 A word search. This word search, unlike others in Books 1 and 2, contains over a hundred words. It is highly unlikely that anyone will ever find all the words, nor are they meant to. If your children find ten or fifteen words, that is quite enough. Most of the words are ones which have been covered in the books and which should, therefore, be familiar to the children.

2 A memory game. The children look at page 23. They should then shut their books and say or draw all that they remember.

3 What's wrong? There is something odd about each of the animals. Children say or write what they think the oddity is, e.g. *The frog has got wings*.

4 Fill in the missing letters. The answers are: BANANA, SNAKE, GIRAFFE, CHICKEN, CROCODILE, ANIMAL, FISH.

5 Find an owl. The children go through the book until they find a picture of an owl. You could vary this by asking them to find other animals, e.g. a caterpillar, a spider, a mouse.

6 Smuff's problem. Smuff can't remember how to get back to his friends. The children find a way through the maze.

Where is the red lizard?
He's trying to blow up Smuff's burrow with dynamited carrots.

A glossary of activities

Blind Man's Buff

- Blindfold one child. Tell the other players that they mustn't speak. They move around the blindfolded child and take turns to shake hands with him or touch him. He tries to guess who the person is by touch alone. This is a useful game for practising **Who?** It can also be adapted for other purposes such as guessing what things are by touch, taste or smell alone.

Chinese Whispers

- Sit the children in a long line close to one another. Whisper a sentence to the first child. He then whispers it to the next child who whispers it to the next, and so on down the line. The last child shouts out the sentence he has heard. Make sure that the children whisper rather than speak aloud, and that they say the sentence once only. You can use this for just about any grammatical structure you wish to practise, and it's fun!

Flashcards

- You can make flashcards, or get the children to make them. Flashcards are pieces of card on which you stick or draw a picture. You can also make flashcards which just have a word on them. They can be used to introduce and practise vocabulary and grammar topics. See also Snap below.

Hangman

- One person, the 'thinker', thinks of a word. He counts up the number of letters in it and draws as many dashes as there are letters. The other players take turns to suggest letters which they think might be in the word. If they are right, the thinker writes the letter in the appropriate place. If they are wrong, he draws one line of a picture of someone hanging from a gallows. Players can try to guess the whole word, but if they are wrong, another line of the picture is drawn. The game continues until the word has been guessed or the picture of the hanged man is finished.

In the Jungle

- The first player says, e.g., *In the jungle I see a lion*. The second player says: *In the jungle I see a lion and a tiger*. The third player says: *In the jungle I see a lion, a tiger and a rabbit*. This game can be played with several people, or just with two. A player who forgets the sequence or gets it wrong drops out. You can adapt this to suit a number of structures, e.g. adjectives, nouns, present continuous.

You can also vary it, like this: *I like cheese. I like cheese and apples. I like cheese, apples and pizza.* OR *In my house there is a cat. In my house there is a cat and a television*. It can equally be played alphabetically, e.g. *Can I have an **a**pple? Can I have an **a**pple and a **b**anana? Can I have an **a**pple, a **b**anana and some **c**risps?*

I Spy

- The first player says, e.g., *I spy with my little eye something beginning with **w*** (a window). Other players have to try to guess what the player has spied. If a player guesses correctly, it is his turn to spy something. Again, this can be played alphabetically. It is a useful game because it can be played anywhere, e.g. on a train, on the way to school, at home, in the garden.

Do you remember?

- For this, you can use pictures in the book, pictures of your own, or objects. Give the players a short time to look at a set of objects on a table, for instance. Now cover them up and see how many of the things they can remember. You can vary this by removing one object at a time and asking what is missing.

Mr Tiger Says

- This game is usually called Simon Says, but since we're in the jungle, it's Mr Tiger. One person is Mr Tiger. He gives orders to the other player(s), e.g. *Mr Tiger says stand up. Mr Tiger says clap your hands*. Players obey his orders unless he doesn't say *'Mr Tiger says'*. If he gives an order like *Sit down* and a player sits, he is out. This is a useful game for practising parts of the body, imperatives and the present continuous.

Pass the Parcel

- Collect lots of used envelopes and scraps of paper. Write a word on each of the scraps of paper. Put one of the bits of paper inside an envelope. Stick the rest of the words to the front of the other envelopes, one on each. Now fold the envelopes and put one inside another until you have a biggish packet. The players sit in a circle and pass the parcel round. Play some music while they are doing this. Stop the music at intervals. The player with the parcel then opens the first envelope. He must make a sentence using the word that is stuck to the front of the envelope. Repeat this until all the envelopes have been opened.

Picture dictation

- One player either thinks of a picture, or uses an existing picture. He describes it slowly to the other players. They draw the things he describes.

Roar, Lion, Roar!

- Blindfold one player. Tell the others to stand near to him. They all make roaring noises like a lion. The teacher or parent then points at one of the players. The others stop making the roaring noises while he continues to roar. The blindfolded player tries to guess who the roarer is. See also Book 1, Chapter 6, 'Longer Activities', for a variation of this game.

Role play

- This is a useful device for practising structures in particular situations. Children and adults take on roles, e.g. shopkeeper and customer; waiter and customer in a restaurant. Props, such as pretend money, will make the role play more realistic and fun.

Snap

- You will have to make sets of cards for this game. Each set of cards must have identical pairs in it. For example, if you wanted to play a game of 'Animal Snap', you would need to make a set of cards which had in it, say, two rabbit cards, two lion cards, two dog cards. If you wanted to practise colours, you would have to make two yellow cards, two red cards, two blue cards etc. You can make these either by drawing them, cutting them out of magazines, or simply writing them. Shuffle the cards and distribute them among the players. Players turn over a card at a time, but they must all do this at the same time. If two cards match, the players shout *Snap!* Whoever shouts *Snap!* first may keep the two cards. The person who runs out of cards first loses.

Treasure Hunt

- Either give the children a list of things to find round the classroom, house, playground or garden, e.g. something blue, a small stick, a big stone, a magazine. Or hide small rewards such as sweets in certain places and give the children clues to help them find them, e.g. *There is something under the bed. There could be something in a cupboard. Have you looked on the bookcase?* This is a good game for practising prepositions and **there is** or **there are**.

True or False?

- Players write or say true and false sentences, either about themselves, or a picture, or their surroundings. The other players have to decide whether the sentences are true or false. This is an excellent way of practising can for ability, **I like** and **I don't like**, **there is** and **there are, this** and **that**, possessives, and many other things.

Word search

- You can make word searches by writing a number of words horizontally and vertically in a square. Disguise the words by adding letters at random at the beginning and end of each word. You can adapt this to suit whatever it is you wish to practise, e.g. you could make a word search entirely composed of animals, colours, nouns, adjectives, verbs.

Yes or No

- One player thinks of a person, an object, an animal or a place. The other player(s) try to guess what he is thinking of by asking questions which can be answered by Yes or No only, e.g. A player thinks of Smuff. Another player asks: *Are you a person?* (No) *Are you an animal?* (Yes) *Do you have a long tail?* (No) *Are you a bird?* (No) *Do you play the bugle?* (Yes).

Oxford University Press, Great Clarendon Street,
Oxford OX2 6DP

Oxford New York
Athens Auckland Bangkok Bogota Bombay
Buenos Aires Calcutta Cape Town Dar es Salaam
Delhi Florence Hong Kong Istanbul Karachi
Kuala Lumpur Madras Madrid Melbourne
Mexico City Nairobi Paris Singapore
Taipei Tokyo Toronto

and associated companies in
Berlin Ibadan

Oxford and Oxford English are trade marks of
Oxford University Press.

ISBN 0 19 431462 6

Cover illustration by Steve Pleydell-Pearce
Design by Samuel T Whistler

Printed in Italy